IS THERE
A GOD?

Richard Swinburne

Revised Edition

OXFORD
UNIVERSITY PRESS

OXFORD
UNIVERSITY PRESS

Great Clarendon Street, Oxford OX2 6DP

Oxford University Press is a department of the University of Oxford.
It furthers the University's objective of excellence in research, scholarship,
and education by publishing worldwide in

Oxford New York

Auckland Cape Town Dar es Salaam Hong Kong Karachi
Kuala Lumpur Madrid Melbourne Mexico City Nairobi
New Delhi Shanghai Taipei Toronto

With offices in

Argentina Austria Brazil Chile Czech Republic France Greece
Guatemala Hungary Italy Japan Poland Portugal Singapore
South Korea Switzerland Thailand Turkey Ukraine Vietnam

Oxford is a registered trade mark of Oxford University Press
in the UK and in certain other countries

Published in the United States
by Oxford University Press Inc., New York

First published 1996
This edition published 2010

British Library Cataloguing in Publication Data

Data available

Library of Congress Cataloging in Publication Data
Library of Congress Control Number 2009938809

Typeset by Laserwords Private Limited, Chennai, India
Printed in Great Britain
on acid-free paper by
Clays Ltd., St Ives plc

ISBN 978–0–19–958043–9

1 3 5 7 9 10 8 6 4 2

ACKNOWLEDGEMENTS

I AM grateful to a number of people who read a first version of *Is There a God?* and helped me to express my ideas in simpler ways than I would otherwise have done; and among them especially Basil Mitchell, Norman Kretzmann, Tim Barton, and Peter Momtchiloff of Oxford University Press, and my daughter Caroline. I am also most grateful to Mrs Anita Holmes for some very fast typing of two versions of the original edition of this book, and to Ms Sarah Barton for typing the new passages inserted into the revised edition.

CONTENTS

INTRODUCTION
TO REVISED EDITION

For the last thirty or forty years there has been a revival of serious debate among philosophers of the English-speaking world about the existence of God. My aim in writing this book (in 1996, and now in 2009 producing a revised edition) has been to put forward for a wider public a short version of the positive case for the existence of God; a case defended at greater length in my book *The Existence of God* (first edition, 1979; second edition, 2004.) The public thinking of recent years about the existence of God has—understandably—been much influenced by the discoveries of modern science about the mechanisms of biological evolution, the development of our universe since the Big Bang thirteen and a half billion years ago, and the possible existence of other universes. But these discoveries leave open the question whether there is a God who caused and sustains the existence and operation of our universe and any other universes there may be in accord with regular processes which scientists are discovering (and occasionally intervenes in those processes); or whether the existence and operation of the universe has no more ultimate explanation.

The basic structure of my argument is this. Scientists, historians, and detectives observe data and proceed thence to some theory about what best explains the occurrence of these data. We can analyse the criteria which they use in reaching a conclusion that a certain theory is better supported by the data than a different theory—that is, is more likely, on the basis of those data, to be true. Using those same criteria, we find that the view that there is a God explains *everything* we observe, not just some narrow range of data. It explains the fact that there is a universe at all, that scientific laws operate within it, that it contains conscious animals and humans with very complex intricately organized bodies, that we have abundant opportunities for developing ourselves and the world, as well as the more particular data that humans report miracles and have religious experiences. In so far as scientific causes and laws explain some of these things (and in part they do), these very causes and laws need explaining, and God's action explains them. The very same criteria which scientists use to reach their own theories lead us to move beyond those theories to a creator God who sustains everything in existence.

Some modern theologians have objected that the concept of God which I develop in Chapter 1 — an essentially all-powerful, all-knowing, and perfectly free person — is not the Christian concept of God, or perhaps even the Jewish or Islamic one; and so they claim that my arguments have no relevance to these religions. This objection has taken two forms. First, they claim that, according to these religions, God is supposed to be totally incomprehensible, whereas I am giving arguments for the existence of a 'God' whom I describe in ordinary words as 'powerful' and 'knowing' things. I do not wish to deny that some words whose meaning we come to understand from their normal use when applied to humans, need to be used in somewhat stretched or analogical senses in order to talk about God — just as 'wave' and 'particle' have to be used in somewhat analogical senses if physicists are to talk about the properties of electrons. Hence my claim (on p. 5) that God is 'in some sense' a person. But the senses can only be *somewhat* analogical. If Christian–Jewish–Islamic tradition really claimed that God was *totally* incomprehensible, and so wasn't in any sense that we could understand 'powerful', or 'knowing', or 'loving' or 'compassionate' or 'merciful', it could not at the same time claim that he had any characteristics which gave us any good reason to worship him. People worship God, among other reasons, because he is supposed to be loving; and we couldn't understand that claim unless God's 'love' was supposed to be something like human love. And anyone who looks at the creeds and doctrinal statements of the Christian tradition of the last two thousand years will see that they describe God as having the properties which I discuss in Chapter 1. In the Christian tradition God is *not* supposed to be totally incomprehensible. The second form of the objection is that the Christian God is supposed to be, not one person, but 'three persons of one substance' (the doctrine of the Trinity), and so my arguments do now show the existence of that God. My arguments are designed to show the existence of a God worshipped alike by Christians, Jews, and Muslims, whom Christian tradition has called 'God the Father'. It is a further claim specific to Christianity that God the Father in virtue of his divine nature brings about 'from all eternity', two other divine persons, the Son and the Holy Spirit, who are so interdependent as to form together one 'God' who is a 'personal being' in a wider sense. It is beyond the scope of this book to discuss that claim, but I discuss it in the companion volume to this book *Was Jesus God?* (published 2008).

This revised edition includes, as well as many very minor corrections, one major correction and one major addition to the text of the original edition. It also includes 'A Guide to Further Reading'. The correction is the rewritten passages on pages 23–4 and 35–40, designed to make clear a distinction between 'full', 'complete' and 'ultimate' explanation ignored in the earlier edition; and thereby to explain better why theism does and materialism does not provide a very simple ultimate explanation of the world. The major addition is a new section on pages 58–62 on the relevance of my argument for God from the fine-tuning of our universe, of the possible existence of many other universes. In order to keep the book of roughly the same length I have omitted a few passages of the original edition which are less central to the argument.

1

GOD

My topic is **the claim that there is a God, understood in** the way
that **Western religion** (Christianity, Judaism, and Islam) has generally
understood that claim. I call that claim theism. In this chapter I shall
spell out what the claim amounts to. Then in later chapters we can
go on to the grounds for believing it to be true. I emphasize that, in
this chapter, when I write that God does this or is like that, I am not
assuming that there is a God, but merely spelling out what the claim
that there is a God amounts to. I am not directly concerned to assess
the claim that there is a God, where 'God' is being understood in some
quite different sense, as the name of a quite different sort of being from
the one worshipped in Western religion. But, in arguing at various
points that theism explains the observed data well, I shall occasionally
point out that other hypotheses, including ones which invoke a 'God' in
some other sense, explain the data less well. Even within the mainstream
of the Western tradition, there have been some differences about what
God is like, and I shall draw attention to some of these differences in
this chapter and suggest that some views about what God is like are to
be preferred to others.

Theism claims that God is a personal being—that is, in some sense
a person. By a person I mean an individual with basic powers (to act
intentionally), purposes, and beliefs.

An **intentional action** is one which a person does and means to
do—as when I walk downstairs or say something which I mean to say.
A basic action is one which a person does intentionally just like that

and not by doing any other intentional action. My going from Oxford to London is a *non-basic action*, because I do it by doing various other actions—going to the station, getting on the train, etc. But squeezing my hand or moving my leg and even saying 'this' are basic actions. I just do them, not by doing any other intentional act. (True, certain events have to happen in my body—my nerves have to transmit impulses—if I am to perform the basic action. But these are not events which I bring about intentionally. They just happen—I may not even know about them.) By a **basic power** I mean a power to perform a basic action. We humans have similar basic powers to each other. They are normally confined to powers of thought and powers over the small chunk of matter, which each of us calls his or her body. I can only produce effects in the world outside my body by doing something intentional with my body. I can open a door by grasping the handle with my hand and pulling it towards me; or I can get you to know something by using my mouth to tell you something. When I produce some effect intentionally (e.g. the door being open) by doing some other action (e.g. pulling it towards me), doing the former is performing a non-basic action. When I go to London, or write a book, or even put a screw into a wall, these are non-basic actions which I do by doing some basic actions. When I perform any intentional action, I seek thereby to achieve some *purpose*—normally one beyond the mere performance of the action itself (I open a door in order to be able to leave the room), but sometimes simply the performance of the action itself (as when I sing for its own sake).

   Beliefs are views, often true but sometimes false, about how the world is. When beliefs are true and well justified, they constitute knowledge. Our human knowledge of the world beyond our bodies is formed by stimuli—of light, sound, smell, and such like—coming from the world beyond our bodies and landing on our bodies. It is because light particles land on our eyes and sound waves (including those produced by speech) land on our ears that we acquire our information about the world. God is supposed to be like us, in having basic powers, beliefs, and purposes—but ones very different from ours. Human persons are either male or female. But the theist, of course, claims that God is neither male nor female. The English language alas does not have a pronoun for referring to persons without carrying any implication of their sex. So I shall follow custom in referring to God as 'he', but I emphasize—without the implication of maleness.

God's basic powers are supposed to be infinite: he can bring about as a basic action any event he chooses, and he does not need bones or muscles to operate in certain ways in order to do so. He can bring objects, including material objects, into existence and keep them in existence from moment to moment. We can imagine finding ourselves having a basic power not merely to move objects, but to create them instantaneously—for example the power to make a pen or a rabbit come into existence; and to keep them in existence and then let them no longer exist. There is no contradiction in this supposition, but of course in fact no human has such a power. What the theist claims about God is that he does have a power to create, conserve, or annihilate anything, big or small. And he can also make objects move or do anything else. He can make them attract or repel each other, in the way that scientists have discovered that they do, and make them cause other objects to do or suffer various things: he can make the planets move in the way that Kepler discovered that they move, or make gunpowder explode when we set a match to it; or he can make planets move in quite different ways, and chemical substances explode or not explode under quite different conditions from those which now govern their behaviour. God is not limited by the laws of nature; he makes them and he can change or suspend them—if he chooses. To use the technical term, God is **omnipotent**: he can do anything.

Human beliefs are limited in their scope, and some of them are true and some of them are false. God is supposed to be **omniscient**—that is, he knows everything. In other words, whatever is true, God knows that it is true. If it snowed on 1 January 10 million BC on the site of present-day New York, God knows that it snowed there and then. If there is a proof of Goldbach's conjecture (something mathematicians have been trying to discover for the past 300 years), God knows what it is; if there is no proof, God knows that there is no proof. All God's beliefs are true, and God believes everything that is true.

Human persons are influenced in forming their purposes by their desires, their in-built inclinations to make this choice and not that one. Our desires include those produced by our bodily physiology—such as desires for food, drink, sleep, and sex—and those formed in part by our culture—such as desires for fame and fortune. We are, it seems to us (I believe, correctly), free to some extent to fight against our desires and do some action other than one which we are naturally inclined to do, but it requires effort. Human beings have limited free will. But God is supposed to be not thus limited. He is **perfectly free**, in that desires never exert causal influence on him at all. Not merely, being omnipotent, can he do whatever he chooses, but he is perfectly free in making his choices.

God then, theism claims, is a person, omnipotent, omniscient, and perfectly free. But now we must be careful how we understand these claims. An **omnipotent** being can do anything. But does that mean that he can make the universe exist and not exist at the same time, make $2 + 2$ to equal 5, make a shape square and round at the same time, or change the past? The majority of religious tradition has claimed that God cannot do these things; not because God is weak, but because the words—for example, 'make a shape square and round at the same time'—do not describe anything which makes sense. There is nothing which would constitute a shape being both square and round. Part of what saying that something is square involves its saying that that thing is not round. So, in technical words, God cannot do what is logically impossible (what involves a self-contradiction). God can make the universe exist and God can make the universe not exist, but God cannot make the universe exist and not exist at the same time. The reason why theists ought to say what I have just said was first grasped clearly by the great Christian philosophical theologian, St Thomas Aquinas, in the thirteenth century.

It seems to me that the same considerations require that we understand God being **omniscient** in a similarly careful way. Just as God cannot be required to do what is logically impossible to do, so God cannot be required to know what is logically impossible to know. It seems to me that it is logically impossible to know (without the possibility of mistake) what someone will do freely tomorrow. If I am really free to choose tomorrow whether I will go to London or stay at home, then if anyone today has some belief about what I will do (e.g. that I will go to London), I have it in my power tomorrow to make that belief false (e.g. by staying at home). So no one (not even God) can know today (without the possibility of mistake) what I will choose to do tomorrow. So I suggest that we understand God being omniscient as God knowing at any time all that is logically possible to know at that time. That will not include knowledge, before they have done it, of what human persons will do freely. Since God is omnipotent, it will only be because God allows there to be free persons that there will be any free persons. So this limit to divine omniscience arises from the consequences (which God could foresee) of his own choice to create free agents. I must, however, warn the reader that this view of mine that God does not know (without the possibility of mistake) what free agents will do until they do it is not the normal Christian (or Jewish or Islamic) view. My view is, however, implied, I believe, by certain biblical passages; it seems, for example, the natural interpretation of the book of Jonah that, when God told Jonah to preach to Nineveh that it would be destroyed, he believed that probably he would need to destroy it, but that fortunately, since the people of Nineveh repented, God saw no need to carry out his prophecy. In advocating this refinement of our understanding of omniscience, I am simply carrying further the process of internal clarification of the basic Christian understanding of God, which other Christian philosophers such as Aquinas pursued in earlier days.

All this does of course assume that **human beings have some limited free will**, in the sense that no causes (whether brain states or God) determine fully how they will choose. That is the way it often seems to us that we have such a power. Even the inanimate world, scientists now realize, is not a fully deterministic world—and the world of thought and choice is even less obviously a predictable world. (I shall have a little more to say about this issue in Chapter 5.)

God—the omnipotent, omniscient, and perfectly free person—is, according to theism, **eternal**. But there are two different ways of understanding 'eternal'. We can understand it, as clearly the biblical writers did, as everlasting: God is eternal in the sense that he has existed at each moment of past time, exists now, and will exist at each moment of future time. Alternatively, we can understand 'eternal' as 'timeless': God is eternal in the sense that he exists outside time. This latter is how all the great philosophical theologians from the fourth to the fourteenth century AD (Augustine, Boethius, and St Thomas Aquinas, for example) understood God's eternity. God does not, on this view, strictly speaking, exist today or yesterday or tomorrow—he just exists. In his one timeless 'moment', he 'simultaneously' causes the events of AD 1995 and of 587 BC. In this one timeless moment also he knows simultaneously (as they happen) what is happening in AD 1995 and in 587 BC. For myself I cannot make much sense of this suggestion—for many reasons. For example, I cannot see that anything can be meant by saying that God knows (as they happen) the events of AD 1995 unless it means that he exists in 1995 and knows in 1995 what is happening then. And then he cannot know in the same act of knowledge (as they happen) the events of 587 BC—for these are different years. Hence I prefer the understanding of God being eternal as his being everlasting rather than as his being timeless. He exists at each moment of unending time.

All the other essential properties which theism attributes to God at each moment of time **follow** from the three properties of omnipotence, omniscience, and perfect freedom. Thus God is supposed to be **bodiless**. For a person to have a body is for there to be a chunk of matter through which alone he or she can make a difference to the physical world and acquire true beliefs about it. But, being omnipotent, God can make differences to the world and learn about it without being thus dependent. So he will have no body; he does not depend on matter to affect and learn about the world. He moves the stars, as we move our arms, just like that—as a basic action. It follows too from his omnipotence that God is **omnipresent** (i.e. present everywhere), in the sense that he can make a difference to things everywhere and know what is happening everywhere just like that, without needing arms or sense organs or the normal operation of light rays in order to do so. But, although he is everywhere present, he is not spatially extended; he does not take up a volume of space—for he has no body. Nor, therefore, does he have any spatial parts: all of him is present everywhere, in the sense in which he is present at a place. It is not that part of him is in England, and another part in the United States.

God being omnipotent could have prevented the universe from existing, if he had so chosen. So it exists only because he allows it to exist. Hence, either he causes the existence of the universe, or he causes or allows some other agent to do so. In this sense, therefore, he is the **creator of the universe**, and, being—by the same argument—equally responsible for its continued existence, he is the sustainer of the universe. He is responsible for the existence of the universe (and every object within it) for as long as it exists. That may be a finite time—the universe may have begun to exist a certain number of years ago; current scientific evidence suggests that the universe began to exist with the 'Big Bang' some 13,500 million years ago. Or the universe may have existed forever. The theist as such is not committed to one or other of these positions. But the theist claims that, even if the universe has existed forever, its existence at each moment of time is due to the conserving action of God at that moment.

God is supposed to be responsible, not merely for the existence of all other objects, but for their having the powers and liabilities they do. Inanimate things have certain powers—for example, to move in certain ways, attract or repel each other. These are not 'basic powers' in the sense in which I was using the term earlier; a basic power is a power to do something intentionally, by choice. The powers of inanimate things are powers to produce effects, but not through choice or for a purpose. In general inanimate things have to act as they do, have to exert their powers under certain circumstances—the gunpowder has to explode when you light it at the right temperature and pressure. That is what I mean by saying that it has a liability to exert its powers under certain circumstances. (On the very small scale, the world is not fully deterministic—atoms and smaller particles have only a probability, a propensity to do this rather than that. Their liability to exert their powers is only a propensity. But this randomness is not a matter of choice, and so their actions are not intentional.) **God**, theism claims, **causes inanimate things to have the powers and liabilities they do, at each moment** when they have them. God continually causes the gunpowder to have the power to explode, and the liability to exercise the power when it is ignited at the right temperature and pressure. And likewise, theism claims, God causes plants and animals (and human bodies, in so far as they act non-intentionally—for example, when the blood is pumped round our arteries and veins) to have the powers and liabilities they do. And God is also responsible for the existence of humans. He could cause us to act of physical necessity. But, given that we have limited free will, **God does not cause us to form the purposes we do**. That is up to us. But God does conserve in us from moment to moment our basic powers to act, and thus ensures that the purposes we form make a difference to the world. God allows us to choose whether to form the purpose of moving a hand or not; and God ensures that (normally), when we form that purpose, it is efficacious—if we try to move our hand, it moves.

When God acts to produce some effect by conserving objects in existence, and conserving their powers and liabilities to act, he produces the effect in a non-basic way. When God makes the gunpowder explode by conserving its explosive power, and its liability to exercise the power when ignited, he produces the explosion in a non-basic way—just as when I cause the door to be open by pulling it towards me. God normally brings about ordinary historical events by these non-basic routes—that is, by making other objects bring about those events. But he could bring about any event by a basic action; and just sometimes, the theist normally claims, he does produce effects in a basic way. He occasionally intervenes in the natural world to produce effects directly—for example, curing someone of cancer, when they would not get better by normal processes. (I shall say more about such divine actions in Chapter 7.)

God is supposed to be **perfectly good**. His being perfectly good follows from his being perfectly free and omniscient. A perfectly free person will inevitably do what he believes to be (overall) the best action and never do what he believes to be an (overall) bad action. In any situation to form a purpose to achieve some goal, to try to achieve some goal involves regarding the goal as in some way a good thing. To try to go to London, I must regard my being in London as in some way a good thing—either because I would enjoy being there, or because thereby I can avoid some unpleasant occasion, or because it is my duty to be in London. To regard some aspect of being in London as good is to have a reason for going to London. If I had no reason at all for going to London, my going there would not be an intentional action (would not be something I meant to do). A person's intentional actions must, therefore, in part be rational; in them he must be guided in part by rational considerations. Yet, as noted earlier, we humans are not fully rational, being subject to desires. (In calling desires non-rational, I do *not* wish to imply that there is something wrong with them, and that we ought not to yield to them. I mean only that they are inclinations with which we find ourselves, not ones solely under the control of reasons.) But a person free from desires who formed his purposes solely on the basis of rational considerations would inevitably do the action which he believed (overall) the best one to do, or (if there is not, the person believes, a best action, but a number of equal best actions) one of the equal best actions.

Now, if there are **moral truths**—truths about what is morally good and bad—an omniscient person will know what they are. If, for example, lying is always morally wrong, God will know that. On the other hand, if lying is wrong only in certain circumstances, then God will know that too. Despite the doubts of the occasional hardened sceptic, we do almost all of us think almost all the time that there are some acts that are morally good (and among them some which are morally obligatory), and some which are morally bad (and among them some which are morally wrong). It is morally good to give (at least some money sometimes) to the starving, and obligatory to feed our own children when they are starving; and it is wrong to torture children for fun. Who can seriously deny these things? The morally good is the overall good. To say that it is morally good to feed the starving is not to say that it is good in all respects; in depriving us of money it may deprive us of some future enjoyment, and so giving will not be good in all respects. But it is good in the more important respect that it saves the lives of human beings and so gives them the opportunity for much future well-being. In consequence, it is overall a good act—or so someone claims who claims that it is a morally good act. God, being omniscient, will have true beliefs about what is morally good, and, being perfectly free, he will do what he believes is (overall) the best. So he will always do what is overall the best, and never do what is overall bad. Hence God will be perfectly good.

Some moral truths are clearly moral truths, whether or not there is a God: it is surely wrong to torture children for fun whether or not there is a God. On the other hand, if theism is true, we owe our existence from moment to moment to the conserving action of God; and he gives us this wonderful world to enjoy. (Of course not all aspects of this world are wonderful, and I will come to consider its bad aspects in Chapter 6.) God is a generous benefactor. One of the most fundamental human obligations (i.e. duties) is (within limits) to please our major benefactors—to do in return for them some small favour which they request in return for the great things they have given us. If theism is true, God is by far our greatest benefactor, for all our other benefactors depend for their ability to benefit us on God's sustaining power. We owe God a lot. Hence **(within limits), if God tells us to do certain things, it becomes our duty to do them**. Just as (within narrow limits) it becomes our duty to do certain things if our parents (when we are children) tell us to do them, or the state tells us to do them, so (within wider limits) it becomes our duty to do things if God tells us to do them. For example, it would not be a duty to worship God especially on Sundays if God did not tell us to do so; but, if God tells us to worship him then, it becomes our duty. (And if his command refers to Saturdays or Fridays instead, then our duty is to worship him then.) And, if God tells us to do something, which is our duty anyway for other reasons (e.g. to ensure that our own children are fed and educated), it becomes even more our duty to do that thing. God is thus a source of moral obligation—his commands create moral obligations. But God clearly cannot make things which are our duty no longer our duty: he cannot make it right to torture children for fun. That being so, it follows from his perfect goodness that he will not command us to do so—for it is wrong to command what is wrong.

It may surprise some modern readers to suppose that a theist can allow that some moral truths are moral truths quite independent of the will of God. This is, however, an issue on which the Christian philosophical tradition has been split right down the middle; and I side with two of its greatest representatives—St Thomas Aquinas and the fourteenth-century Scottish philosopher Duns Scotus—in holding that there are moral truths independent of the will of God. God can only enforce these, not alter them. But, if there are moral truths such as 'it is wrong to torture children for fun', which hold independently of the will of God, they will be like 'no shape can be both round and square at the same time'; they must hold whatever the world is like, and that is because there is no sense ultimately in supposing them not to hold.

Good actions are of two kinds. There are **obligations** (i.e. duties), and there are good actions beyond obligation—called **supererogatory good actions**. We are blameworthy if we fail to fulfil our obligations but normally not praiseworthy for fulfilling them. Conversely, no blame attaches to us if we fail to do some supererogatory good act, but we are praiseworthy if we do it. Just where the line is to be drawn is not always obvious. But it is clear that there is a line. If I borrow money, I have an obligation to repay. If I fail to repay borrowed money, I am blameworthy; but I do not normally deserve any praise for repaying the money. Conversely, I have no obligation to throw myself on a grenade that is about to explode in order to save the life of a friend who is standing close. But if I do the action, I deserve the highest praise. Obligations mostly arise from benefits voluntarily accepted or undertakings voluntarily entered into. I have no obligation to marry and have children; but, if I do have children, I have an obligation to feed and educate them. This suggests that God before he creates any other persons has no obligations, though it is a supererogatory good act for him to create many other persons including humans. If he does create them, he will then incur certain obligations towards them. Exactly what those are may be disputed, but the Christian tradition has normally maintained, for example, that, if God makes promises to us, he is obliged to keep them.

To fail to fulfil your obligations is always an overall bad act, but obligations are limited. God can easily, and in virtue of his perfect goodness will easily, fulfil all his obligations. But there is no limit to the possible acts of supererogatory goodness which a person can do except any limit arising from his or her powers. We humans have limited powers; and can do only a few limited supererogatory good acts. I can give my savings to one charity, but then I will be unable to give anything to another charity. If I devote my life to caring for one group of children in England, I shall be unable to care for another group of children in a distant land. God's powers, however, are unlimited. But even God, we have seen, cannot do the logically impossible. And it is logically impossible to do every possible supererogatory good act. It is good that God should create persons, including human persons. But, however many he creates, it would be even better if he created more (perhaps well spaced out in an infinitely large universe). Given that human life is in general a good thing, the more of it the better. God cannot create the best of all possible worlds, for there can be no such world—any world can be improved by adding more persons to it, and no doubt in plenty of other ways as well. So what does **God's perfect goodness** amount to? Not that he does all possible good acts—that is not logically possible. Presumably that he fulfils his obligations, does no bad acts, and performs very many good acts.

So God's perfect goodness places very little restriction on which actions he will do. The restriction that he must perform no bad acts, and so fulfil all his obligations, may limit somewhat what he can do with creatures while he keeps them in being. But it does not, I suggest, oblige him to keep them in being forever (good though it is in some cases that he should), let alone create them in the first place. But there is open to God an infinite range of good acts: infinitely many different universes which he could create, and infinitely many different things he could do with them—all possible expressions of creative overflowing love. Yet, although there are infinitely many different universes he could create, there are perhaps only a small number of *kinds* of universe he could create. He could create universes containing some persons of limited powers such as humans, or universes without such persons. And the obvious goodness of at least one universe of the former kind makes it quite likely that he will create one. But there is no limit to the possibilities of how many persons it could contain, and indeed which persons they are. God must choose which to do of the infinitely many good actions, each of which he has a reason to do. So, like ourselves in a situation where we have a choice between actions, each of which we have equal reason to do, God must perform a 'mental toss-up'—decide, that is, on which reason to act in a way which is not determined by his nature or anything else. We can understand such an operation of non-determined rational choice, for we seem sometimes to experience it in ourselves.

So it follows from God being everlastingly omnipotent, omniscient, and perfectly free that he is an everlastingly bodiless, omnipresent, creator and sustainer of the universe, perfectly good, and a source of moral obligation. But theism does not claim merely that the person who is God has these properties of being everlastingly omnipotent, omniscient, and perfectly free. It claims that God has these properties necessarily—these are **essential properties of God**. Let me explain what this means. Every object has some essential properties and some accidental (i.e. non-essential) properties. The essential properties of an object are those which it cannot lose without ceasing to exist. One of the essential properties of my desk, for example, is that it occupies space. It could not cease to occupy space (become disembodied) and yet continue to exist. By contrast, one of its accidental properties is being brown. It could still exist if I painted it red so that it was no longer brown. Persons are essentially objects with the potential to have (intentional) powers, purposes, and beliefs. I may be temporarily paralysed and unconscious and so have temporarily lost the power to think or move my limbs. But, if I lose the potential to have these powers (if I lose them beyond the power of medical or other help to restore them), then I cease to exist. On the other hand, my powers can grow or diminish, and my beliefs can change (I can forget things I once knew, and acquire new areas of knowledge), while the same I continues to exist through all the change.

By contrast, theism maintains that the personal being who is God cannot lose any of his powers or knowledge or become subject to influence by desire. If God lost any of his powers, he would cease to exist, just as my desk would cease to exist if it ceased to occupy space. And eternity (that is, everlastingness) also being an essential property of God means that no individual who had begun to exist or could cease to exist would be God.

If, as theism maintains, there is a God who is essentially eternally omnipotent, omniscient, and perfectly free, then he will be **the ultimate brute fact** which explains everything else. God is responsible for the existence of everything else besides himself and for it being as it is and having the powers and liabilities it does; by his continual action at each moment of time, God's own existence is the only thing whose existence God's action does not explain. For that there is no explanation. In that sense God is a necessary being, something which exists under its own steam, not dependent on anything else.

So that is the God whom theists (Christian, Jewish, and Islamic among others) claim to exist. Why should we believe them? To answer that question we must look at the criteria which scientists, historians and others use when they put forward their theories about the causes of what they observe.

2

HOW WE EXPLAIN THINGS

Two Kinds of Explanation

The world consists of objects—or, more technically, as philosophers sometimes call them, substances. Desks and trees, stars and galaxies, atoms and electrons, animals and human beings are all **substances**. (I must warn the reader that I am using the word 'substance' not as the name of a kind of thing—such as oil or sulphur—but as the name of individual things. It is this desk or that tree which is a substance.) Substances have **properties**: they are square or have such and such a mass or electric charge; and they have **relations** to other substances: one substance is 10 feet away from some other substance or to the left of it, exists earlier than it, or looks yellow to it. A substance having a property (this desk having a mass of 10 kg) or relation (the desk standing on the floor), or changing its properties (this lump of putty changing from being square to being round) or relations (me moving away from you), or coming into existence or ceasing to exist is an **event** (or phenomenon). Events are caused by substances. The dynamite caused the explosion, one billiard ball caused another to move away, and the marksman caused the motion of the gun trigger. Often many substances combine to cause some event. Several painters may combine to cause a house to be painted, and sun and earth may both exert force on the moon so as to cause it to move in a certain path.

Human beings have always sought the true explanations of all the events (all the phenomena) of which they know, have sought to discover the causes of events and the reasons why those causes had the effects they did. We have had practical aims in this: if we know what causes explosions or the growth of plants, then we can bring these things about ourselves. But humans have also had deep non-practical aims in finding out the causes of things and the reasons why the causes produced the effects they did—both the causes of particular things (what made the President or the Prime Minister say what he did), and of very general things (what causes leaves to be green, or animals to exist; and how do they cause these effects).

We find **two different kinds of explanations of events**, two different ways in which objects cause events. There is inanimate causation, and there is intentional causation. When the dynamite causes a particular explosion, it does so because it has, among its properties, the power to do so and the liability to exercise that power under certain conditions—when it is ignited at a certain temperature and pressure. It has to cause the explosion under those conditions; it has no option, and there is nothing purposive about it doing so. But the dynamite was ignited because, say, a terrorist ignited it. The terrorist caused the ignition, because he had the power to do so, the belief that doing so would cause an explosion, and the purpose of causing an explosion. He chose to cause the ignition; he could have done otherwise. Here we have two kinds of explanation. The first, in terms of powers and liabilities, is **inanimate explanation**. The second, in terms of powers, beliefs, and purposes, is intentional, or—as I shall call it in future—**personal explanation**. Different phenomena are explained in different ways: some events are brought about intentionally by persons (and animals, some of whom also act intentionally), and some events are brought about by inanimate things.

The personal-explanation model of explanation is, like the inanimate one, unavoidable in our thinking about the world. Some thinkers have claimed that persons and their purposes really make no difference to what happens; brain events cause and are caused by other nerve events and bring about bodily movements without persons and purposes making any difference. But no one can think consistently in that way. To form a purpose (in the sense which I have described) to move one's hand or whatever involves trying to move the hand. And we know very well that, if we ceased to form purposes and to try to execute them, nothing would happen; we would cease to eat and talk and write and walk as we do. What we try to achieve makes all the difference to what happens.

Scientists refine our ordinary everyday explanations of events. Physics and chemistry provide inanimate explanations, and so much history, psychology, sociology, and detective work provide personal explanations. We find that **inanimate objects of similar kinds all have similar powers, and similar liabilities** to exercise those powers under different conditions. It is not merely that heating a particular piece of copper causes it to expand, but that all copper expands when heated. These generalizations about when things exercise their powers are called **laws of nature**, or natural laws, or scientific laws. Psychologists and sociologists have not so far been nearly as successful at finding generalizations about human purposive behaviour. But no doubt there are some generalizations to be found about which human persons have which powers and beliefs under which circumstances; and, to some extent, about which purposes they will probably (though not certainly) form.

If every object in the world had different powers and liabilities (to exercise them under certain conditions) from every other one, the world would be a very complicated and unpredictable place. But it is a fortunate fact, which I shall be going on to emphasize quite a lot, that objects fall into kinds whose members all behave in the same way. All volumes of water freeze at the same temperature—that is, they have the power to freeze, and the liability to exercise that power when the temperature falls to $0°C$. All electrons (the particles of electric charge) repel all other electrons with the same force in all conditions. And so on and so on. And it seems that all material objects whatsoever conform to the same very general laws of behaviour—for example, each attracts each other with a gravitational force which (to a high degree of accuracy) Newton codified in his law of gravitational attraction. Scientists are trying to find the most general laws of nature from which all the lesser laws applying only very approximately, or applying only to special kinds of objects (water, or electrons), apply. In discussing the laws of nature, what scientists are discussing are the powers and liabilities to act of innumerable particular substances, either all particular objects or ones of certain kinds.

Because of this widespread uniformity in the behaviour of things, we may phrase our explanation of a particular event in terms of the initial conditions surrounding the causing substance which triggered it to act, and a law of nature stating what powers and liabilities substances of that kind have. We may say that the copper expanded because the copper was heated and it is a law of nature that all copper expands when heated. But it is important to bear in mind that laws of nature are not substances; they are just human summaries of the powers and liabilities of substances. It is the powers and liabilities of a particular piece of copper which make it expand when heated. While I shall need to come back to this point, I shall find it more convenient for much of the rest of this chapter to summarize **inanimate explanation** simply as **initial conditions plus law of nature causing event**.

Explanations in the physical sciences are, of course, normally a lot more complicated than the (over-simplified) example of the last paragraph. They typically involve several initial conditions and several different laws. An explanation of Jupiter being where it is now may involve the positions of Jupiter and the sun last year and also those of other planets, and several laws (such as Newton's three laws of motion and his law of gravitational attraction), and the process of deriving from these the phenomenon to be explained may be quite a lengthy one. The explanation will be a true one if the suggested initial conditions did indeed occur, the cited laws are indeed true laws, and together these lead us to expect Jupiter to be where it is.

Laws of nature may be universal ones (e.g. 'all particles of light travel with a velocity of 300,000 km/sec.') or statistical ones ('all atoms of radium have a probability of $\frac{1}{2}$ of decaying within 1,620 years').

The factors involved in explanation can themselves often be explained. The position of Jupiter last year can be explained in terms of its position the year before; and the operation of Newton's laws of motion can be explained by the operation of more general laws—for example, Einstein's laws. (That is, the powers and liabilities to act, which a substance has as described by Newton's laws, are derived from the ones it has as described by Einstein's laws.) Typically, low-level laws concerned with things readily observable (e.g. volumes of a gas in a test tube) in some narrow region (e.g. near the surface of the earth) are explained by 'higher-level' laws which concern the behaviour of things not so readily observable (the molecules or atoms of gases) over a wider region. Similarly, to revert to personal explanation, some powers, purposes and beliefs may be explained by other purposes and beliefs. I form a purpose of going to the cupboard because I have the purpose of getting food and I believe that there is food in the cupboard.

By a '**full explanation**' of an event I mean one which is such that given the substances and the conditions in which they occur, their powers and liabilities to act (or beliefs and purposes), which the explanation cites, the event must inevitably occur. To use the terminology of 'laws of nature', full inanimate explanations of an event by laws of nature and initial conditions entail its occurrence. By a '**partial explanation**' of an event I mean one which makes the occurrence of the event only probable; this may be because it does not mention all the substances, etc. involved in the causal process, or because the substances involved have only a probabilistic liability to produce the event in question. (For example, as I noted, an atom of radium only has a probability of $\frac{1}{2}$ to decay within 1,620 years.) By a '**complete explanation**' of an event I mean a full explanation, which cites causes with their most fundamental powers and liabilities (or beliefs and purposes). To use the terminology of 'laws of nature', complete inanimate explanations will invoke the most fundamental laws. If the operation of Einstein's laws is explained by the operation of the laws of a Grand Unified theory and the latter have no further explanation, then it is these latter which form part of a complete inanimate explanation. A complete personal explanation will invoke powers, beliefs, and purposes which do not derive from simultaneous higher-level powers, purposes, and beliefs. Thus if I go to the larder because I have the purpose of getting food, and I have the purpose of getting food because I have the purpose of eating regular meals but my having this latter purpose does not have a further explanation in terms of a wider purpose of mine, then it is the latter and not the former purpose which forms part of a complete explanation of my going to the larder.

The Justification of Explanation

So much for the elements involved in explanation of the two kinds: inanimate substances, and their powers, liabilities, and events which trigger them off; persons, and their powers, purposes, and beliefs. These are the causes of events and the reasons why the causes have the effects they do. But what justifies a claim that so and so is the cause of some event and such and such is the reason why it had the effect it did? Let us answer this question first for inanimate explanation, and let us continue to operate temporarily in terms of laws of nature and initial conditions. Why do we suppose, for example, that Newton's laws of motion and the previous positions of sun, moon, and other planets explain the present position of Jupiter?

A claim that some proposed law is really a law of nature, is justified (i.e. likely to be true, rendered probable) **to the extent to which**:

(1) It leads us to expect (with accuracy) many and varied events which we observe (and we do not observe any events whose non-occurrence it leads us to expect).

(2) What is proposed is simple.

(3) It fits well with our background knowledge.

(4) We would not otherwise expect to find these events (e.g. there is no rival law which leads us to expect these events which satisfies criteria (1–3) as well as does our proposed law).

Let me illustrate these criteria at work with a somewhat simplified version of a famous historical case. Consider Kepler in the sixteenth century studying the motion of the planet Mars. Others have provided him with a large number of observations of past positions of Mars. He wishes to discover the law governing the movement of Mars—that is, the path along which Mars moves, knowledge of which will enable him to predict its future positions. He can mark on a map of the sky the observed past positions, and clearly any law governing the motion of Mars will be represented by a curve which passes through those positions (approximately—there may be small inaccuracies of observation). Such a law will satisfy Criterion 1. The trouble is that **an infinite number of different curves will satisfy Criterion 1**. One possibility is, of course, that Mars moves in an ellipse. Another is that Mars moves in a spiral which diverges hardly at all from the ellipse during the period studied so far, but will diverge significantly hereafter. Another is that Mars moves along a path which describes increasingly large ellipses which eventually become parabolic in shape. Then there are curves of a kind marked in Figure 1, coinciding with the ellipse for the observations made so far but diverging subsequently in a quite wild way. How is a choice to be made? Most possible curves are very un-simple in two respects—their equations are highly complex and their graphical representation is unsmooth. The equation of an ellipse is relatively simple, and the curve is smooth. Some other rivals are perhaps almost equally simple, and we may not be able to decide between them and the ellipse until we have more observations, or we may be able to do so by some other criterion. But, for the serious work of eliminating almost all

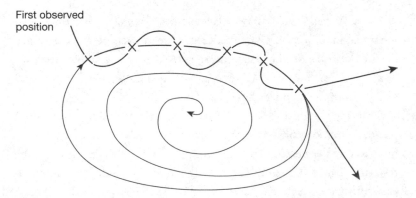

Figure 1 Possible curves for the motion of Mars (positions of Mars marked by crosses)

of the infinite number of other alternatives, **Criterion 2**—the criterion
of **simplicity**—**is essential**.

Criterion 3 does, however, also come in—the proposed law has to
fit well with our **background knowledge**. By 'background knowledge'
I mean knowledge of how things work in neighbouring areas. For
example, when we are considering theories about how a particular gas
behaves at low temperature, we take into account what, if anything,
we know about how other gases behave at low temperature. Our third
criterion is satisfied to the extent to which a proposed law 'fits' with
that wider knowledge. In plotting his curve for Mars, Kepler took into
account his knowledge of how other planets behaved. If the law of
planetary motion best justified for Mercury, Venus, Jupiter, and Saturn
had not been that of an ellipse, but, say, that of a spiral, then, although
a spiral law may be less simple than that of an ellipse, Kepler would have
had good grounds for preferring it to the ellipse as the law governing the
motion of Mars. In fact, of course, Kepler found that for other planets
also the suggested law that best satisfied the other criteria was the law
that the planet moves in an ellipse. In each case there was no further
background knowledge to take into account than that of the motions
of other planets, and so Kepler could adduce as the law of planetary
motion, not merely for Mars but for all planets, that they move in
ellipses.

However well some proposed law satisfies Criteria 1–3, if there is an
incompatible law which satisfies those criteria even better, since they
cannot both be laws, the former must be rejected. That is what Criterion
4 says. No rival law proposed for Mars satisfied Criteria 1–3 better, and
so the law of the ellipse satisfied **Criterion 4**.

Scientific laws fit together into scientific theories. Kepler's theory of
planetary motion consisted of three laws, of which we have had time to
discuss only the first. But the same criteria come into play to judge the
resulting theory. The simplicity of a theory will include its component
laws fitting together well. As we noted earlier, laws and so theories can
be explained by higher-level theories. The same criteria are again at
work. The operation of Kepler's laws is explained by the operation of

Newton's laws, given that the mass of the sun is large in comparison to that of the planets. The grounds for believing Newton's theory to be true are (Criterion 1) that we can derive from it well-justified laws of nature in many diverse fields—Kepler's laws, Galileo's law of fall, laws of the motions of planetary moons, tides, pendula, and so on—which (Criterion 4) we would have no other reason to expect to hold. Newton's three laws of motion and his law of gravitational attraction are simple (Criterion 2)—in comparison with wild alternatives which could be constructed.

The criterion of background knowledge (Criterion 3) does not operate when we do not have knowledge of how things work in any neighbouring fields of enquiry. If we do not have any measurements of the positions of other planets, let alone any postulated laws of their behaviour, we cannot take into account the behaviour of other planets in assessing a theory about the behaviour of Mars. And, inevitably, the wider our area of enquiry, the less there will be any neighbouring fields to take into account. In his theory of mechanics Newton was trying to explain so much that (since so little was known in the seventeenth century about chemistry, light, and electromagnetism) there was no neighbouring area with which he could compare his own area. He justified his theory on the grounds that it was a simple theory which led him to expect the observed phenomena which otherwise would not be expected. And clearly, **where we are concerned with explaining (literally) everything observed, the criterion of background knowledge will be irrelevant.**

Anyway, **Criterion 3 reduces to Criterion 2.** For what is it for one law to 'fit' with another? Kepler's laws for the motion of Mars fitted with his laws for the motion of the other planets because they had the same form. But what this amounts to is that the combination of laws—'the other planets move always in an ellipse and Mars moves always in an ellipse'—was to be preferred to 'the other planets move always in an ellipse and Mars moves always in a spiral'. Why? Because the first supposition is simpler than the second. It can be phrased simply as 'all planets move always in ellipses'. In other words, a law for a narrow area fits well with laws of a neighbouring area, in so far as they support a simple rather than a complex law for the whole area. Because the criterion of background knowledge in judging the acceptability of a proposed narrow law in the end boils down to the criterion of simplicity for a wider law, I shall often be able to ignore it in future. It is **simplicity** which is the key criterion for judging between laws which yield the observed data.

A reader may think that we could eliminate all these 'wild' curves which are compatible with observations by waiting for more observations. Will not the next observation of a position of Mars eliminate all the curves which I have marked on my diagram (Figure 1) except one—presumably the ellipse? Yes, but there will still be an infinite number of curves (which I had no space to mark on the diagram) which pass through the old positions and the new one and yet diverge wildly in the future. Without the criterion of simplicity, we never have any way of choosing between an infinite number of theories compatible with data. Some writers claim that our preference for simplicity is a mere matter of convenience, that we prefer simpler theories because they are easy to operate with; our preference for simplicity has nothing to do with an interest in truth. That seems false. Often we need predictions about the future; they are crucial for our survival as well as for fulfilling more ambitious plans. We need to know whether the bridge will break if we drive a lorry over it, whether the drug will kill or cure, whether the nuclear explosion will set up a chain reaction which will destroy all humanity, and so on. We get our predictions by using the simplest theory which extrapolates from past observations; and we believe that the predictions of such a theory are more probably true than those of any other theory. If we really thought that the predictions of all theories (which yielded observations made so far) were equally likely to be true, we would never be justified in relying on one rather than another. Yet we do rely on one rather than another, and think that we are justified in doing so, and that can only be because we regard the simplicity of a theory as crucial evidence of its truth.

The 'simplicity' of a scientific theory is a matter of it having few component laws, each of which relates few variables by mathematically simple formulae (whose consequences for observation are derivable by mathematically simple steps). If a theory postulates objects or properties beyond those which we can observe (such as atoms and electrons, quarks or quasars), the criterion of simplicity tells us to postulate few new objects, few new kinds of objects, few new properties, and few new kinds of property—and the fewer the better. The rule that you should postulate no more new objects than you need to explain your observations is often called 'Ockham's razor'. But how you apply it depends on what you understand by 'need'. It is, of course, right to postulate a *few* objects, if they provide an explanation of *many* phenomena. It may sometimes seem to non-scientists that scientists put forward some pretty un-simple theories. Einstein's General Theory of Relativity does not look very simple, but his claim for it was that it was the simplest among theories which yielded the data of observation. The simplest theory for some area which satisfies Criterion 1 may not be very simple, but it may still be far simpler than an infinite number of possible theories which satisfy Criterion 1 equally well.

To return briefly to Criterion 1—note that it, like the other **criteria, can be satisfied to different degrees**. It is satisfied to the extent to which a law or theory leads us to expect many events. The more it can explain, the better. The more varied events it can explain, the better. A theory which can explain phenomena in different areas is to be preferred to one which can explain phenomena only in one area. A theory is better in so far as it can explain phenomena accurately; that is, the theory leads us to expect a phenomenon described in a certain way, and a phenomenon exactly as described is observed. But if what is observed is not quite what the theory leads us to expect—for example, the theory predicts that the planet will be at an angle of celestial longitude $106°1'2''$, and it is observed at an angle of $106°2'12''$—to the extent of approximately $1'$ the theory is inaccurate. The theory may still be correct because the observations may be slightly inaccurate or because factors of which we do not know may have affected the outcome, but the less need there is to postulate such errors, the more reason there is to believe the theory to be true. And, finally, a law which leads us to expect what is observed with only some probability is less well justified than one which leads us to expect what is observed with certainty. All these are aspects of Criterion 1.

I have not so far spoken of scientific laws or theories 'predicting' observations, merely of them 'leading us to expect observations', because talk of **prediction** (in the analysis of Criterion 1 and other criteria) might suggest that observations provide evidence for a theory only if first the theory is formulated, then the scientist works out what the theory leads us to expect in the future, and then he observes what it leads us to expect. But I cannot see that it matters as regards the support given by observations to the theory whether, say, 100 observations are made first and the theory then constructed to explain them, or whether the theory is constructed on the basis of fifty observations and it successfully predicts another fifty. The support given by observations to a theory concerns a logical relation between observations and the theory, and is independent of when the observations are made. Those who think otherwise say that theories can always be constructed to fit observations, whereas theories do not always predict accurately; and so accurate prediction provides a more objective test of a proposed theory. Certainly theories can always be constructed to fit observations, but what cannot always be constructed are simple theories which yield many observations. They are just as difficult to find as theories which predict accurately, and they are the only ones which observations support. An example to illustrate the irrelevance to theory-support of *when* the observations are made is provided by Newton's theory of motion. This was judged by many (surely correctly) to be highly probable on the evidence available to scientists of the early eighteenth century, even though it made no predictions which could be tested for many years, other than the predictions which were already made by laws which were already known and which Newton's theory purported to explain (e.g. Kepler's laws of planetary motion and Galileo's law of fall). The high probability of Newton's theory arose solely from its being a very simple higher-level theory from which those diverse laws are deducible.

I have made this point at a little length because it is often claimed that theism and fuller theological theories do not make 'predictions' which can readily be tested. (They may make predictions about life after death, for example, but those cannot readily be tested now.) What I have argued, and what the history of science shows, is that theories are well established if they lead us to expect observations, whether the observations are new ones or old ones; and I shall be arguing that theism is a very simple theory which leads us to expect very many old observations. This point being made, I shall in future sometimes talk of theories 'predicting' observations, meaning thereby just that they lead us to expect observations, without any implication about whether the observations were made before or after the postulation of the theory.

So these, then, are the four criteria at work for judging the probability of some scientific theory being true and so contributing to the true explanation of some event. Now **the laws** of scientific theories **are simply regularities in the powers and liabilities of particular substances**. That all planets move in ellipses round the sun is just the regularity that each planet has the power to move in an ellipse and the liability to exercise that power when the sun is at the focus of the ellipse. What the scientist discovers by means of his criteria are the powers and liabilities to act of particular substances, and he seeks the simplest account of these which will enable him to make successful predictions.

A true explanation of an event will involve not only the correct scientific theory, but also **correctly described initial conditions** (i.e. which substances there were in what conditions). What explains the present position of the planet Uranus is not just Newton's theory but also the past positions of the sun, Uranus, and other planets. How do we know what these were? We may have observed them. Or, if not, the hypothesis that there were planets in such and such positions may provide the best explanation of phenomena which we do observe. And by 'best explanation' I mean explanation which satisfies best our four criteria. We may try to explain the present position of Uranus in terms of Newton's laws, and the past positions of the sun and Uranus and of the other planets that we can observe. But, if all that does not lead us to expect exactly what we observe, we may postulate (as Leverrier did in 1846) that there is another planet, Neptune, beyond Uranus, which we cannot observe, pulling Uranus out of orbit. If we cannot see this planet, what are the grounds for supposing that it is there? One powerful ground is that otherwise we will have to abandon Newton's theory, which, unless we postulate Neptune, would be unable to predict the behaviour of Uranus. That is, the simplest account of a vast number of phenomena is that Newton's theory is true and that the heavenly bodies include Neptune. Further grounds for asserting the existence of Neptune would be provided if the supposition of its existence would explain other otherwise inexplicable phenomena. In postulating unobservable entities we postulate those entities and that scientific theory (about the powers and liabilities to act of objects) which together best satisfy our four criteria. As I noted earlier, one facet of simplicity is to postulate few objects. If postulating one unobservable planet suffices to lead us to expect the observations we find, we must not postulate two.

The same four criteria are at work in judging the worth of personal explanations. In explaining some phenomena as caused by persons, we seek a hypothesis which leads us to expect the phenomena which we would not otherwise expect to find, as simple a hypothesis as possible, and one which fits in with background knowledge. Suppose that we find among pages recovered from an ancient library three pages of an apparently connected philosophical argument in the same handwriting. One hypothesis is that the same person wrote all three pages. An alternative hypothesis is that each page was written by a different philosopher at a different time; all three philosophers had identical handwriting; but only the first page of the first philosopher's text, the second page of the second philosopher's text, and the third page of the third philosopher's text have survived; although the arguments were different from each other, coincidentally the three pages fit together to make an argument which none of them was putting forward. While this latter hypothesis satisfies Criterion 1 (of predicting the observations) as well as does the former hypothesis, clearly it satisfies the criterion of simplicity far less well—for it postulates many persons, purposes, and beliefs, rather than one person, one purpose, and one set of beliefs. Background knowledge will also enter into the assessment of such hypotheses—knowledge, for example, about whether people often have identical handwriting and whether different pages of different argument(s) often fit together to make an apparently connected argument(s).

In assessing a much wider range of phenomena in terms of their causation by human persons we build up a picture of the phenomena as caused by as few persons with as constant powers and purposes and beliefs which change in regular ways (e.g. in response to various sensory stimuli) as we can. If we can explain two effects brought about by a human in terms of the same purpose, we do not invoke a quite new purpose to explain the second effect. If we can explain an effect as brought about by a person in virtue of powers of the same kind as other humans have, we do not postulate some novel power—we do not postulate that a person has a basic power of bending spoons at some distance away if we can explain the phenomenon of the spoons being bent by someone else bending them with his hands. And so on.

Just as we may need to postulate unobservable planets and atoms to explain phenomena, so **we may need to postulate non-embodied persons** if such an explanation of the phenomena satisfies the four criteria better. If the contents of my room start flying around and form themselves into words, the best explanation may be in terms of the action of a poltergeist with certain basic powers other than normal human powers (basic powers over objects within a certain region, say), purposes, and beliefs. Also, it may not always be obvious when a body is the body of a person, and so that the movements of some part of it are brought about intentionally. Suppose we travel to a distant planet and find there moving objects with appendages. Are these bodies of persons, or merely inanimate things? Our answer will depend on whether we can explain vast numbers of their movements and those of their appendages by supposing that they are persons with certain basic powers (of control over their appendages), (constant) purposes, and beliefs (acquired in a certain regular way).

The four criteria are at work to determine which of all our many claims about the world beyond observation are most likely to be true. In all fields we seek the simplest hypothesis which leads us to expect the phenomena we find (and which, if there is background knowledge, fits best with it).

3

THE SIMPLICITY OF GOD

Ultimate Explanation

Inanimate and personal causation interact. Sometimes one explains the existence and operation of the factors involved in the other. Physical science explains why a ball dropped from a tower 64 feet above the ground takes two seconds to reach the ground. But we may require a personal explanation of why the ball was dropped at all. It might be that Galileo dropped it in order to test his proposed law of gravity. Conversely, clearly human powers, beliefs, and purposes are causally affected by inanimate factors. My beliefs may be caused by the arrival of light rays on my eyes and sound waves on my ears. The process of belief-production does not involve the light rays having any purpose to cause my beliefs: the process is analysable in terms of the powers and liabilities of inanimate objects—at least partially. Likewise, my basic powers of bodily movement are caused by the states of my nerves and brain—at least partially. I can move my arm when I choose only if my brain, nerves, muscles, and so on are in certain states. Their being in the requisite state is part of the cause of my having the power to move my arm. The way I do move my arm intentionally is by (unintentionally) causing a brain state which in turn causes the arm movement. Also, my purposes are formed under the influence of desires having their origin in the state of my body—my desire to eat, for example, being caused by the emptiness of my stomach. (My view in the case of purposes, as I stated earlier, is that such influences are only partial. A person has the power to resist such influences.) Inanimate and personal causation interact. Inanimate factors help to form our choices; our choices help to form the inanimate world.

The reader will recall that by a 'complete explanation' of an event, I mean a full explanation which involves substances with their powers and liabilities etc. described in the most fundamental way. If the complete explanation cites persons, their powers, beliefs and purposes, then that explanation is a personal explanation. If it cites inanimate substances, their powers and liabilities (or, in other words, laws of nature), the complete explanation is an inanimate one. But we often look for more than just any complete explanation of an event; we want not just a complete explanation in terms of factors operating at the time of the occurrence of the event to produce that event, but one which explains in terms of earlier causes why those factors, which operated at the time of the occurrence of the event to produce that event, existed in the first place. We want to know what at an earlier time caused me to exist and have the powers, beliefs, and purposes which I have; what at an earlier time caused the light-rays to land on my eyes, or caused the emptiness of my stomach. A complete explanation of some events in which all the factors involved have no further explanation, full or partial, in terms of earlier causes constitutes what I shall call an **ultimate explanation** of the event.

The human quest for explanation inevitably and rightly seeks for an ultimate explanation of everything observable—that substance or substances on which everything else depends for its existence and properties. Not everything will have an explanation. A may be explained by B, and B by C, but in the end there will be some one substance or many substances with such and such properties on which all other objects depend. We will have to acknowledge *something* as ultimate—the great metaphysical issue is *what* that is. There seem to be three possible ultimate explanations available. One is **materialism**. What I mean by this is the view that the existence and operation of all the factors involved in personal explanation have a complete inanimate explanation. It is not the extreme—and to my mind obviously false—view that persons, their beliefs, purposes, and so on just *are* material objects and their physical states. That view seems obviously false—someone's purpose to conquer the world is not the same event as some nerve firing in the brain. A list of the events occurring in the world which included only the latter and not the former would have left something out. A Martian who discovered everything about my brain would still want to know whether I had purposes or was just an inanimate robot. (I shall have more to say about this point in Chapter 5.) What I mean here by materialism is the view that the personal and mental, though distinct from it, are fully caused by the physical; that the existence of persons, and their having the purposes, powers, and beliefs they do, has a inanimate explanation (in terms of the powers and liabilities of such material objects as nerve cells). It may be that as we explain the whole state of the universe, we come eventually to a first state of affairs, a first chunk of matter with the power to produce all subsequent matter and the liability to do so at some time or other. This first state would by itself provide an ultimate explanation of everything. Alternatively the chain of explanation may go back forever; today's state of the universe is explained by yesterday's state, and yesterday's state by the state of the universe the day before yesterday, and so on forever. In that case—on the materialist view—any ultimate explanation of the universe will include a whole beginningless earlier state of the universe—all the substances with their powers and liabilities existing at all earlier times, taken together.

One alternative to materialism is a mixed theory—that the existence and operation of the factors involved in personal explanation do not all have an ultimate explanation in inanimate terms; and, conversely, that the existence and operation of the factors involved in inanimate explanation do not all have an ultimate explanation in personal terms. Let us call this theory humanism.

The third possibility is that the existence and operation of the factors involved in inanimate explanation are themselves to be explained in personal terms, where persons include, not just human persons, but persons of other kinds. One theory of this type, **theism**, is the view that there is a God. On this view, as we saw in Chapter 1, God keeps in existence the material objects of our universe from moment to moment, with their powers and liabilities to act. He acts on the world, as we act on our bodies; but, unlike us, he is not dependent on any body for his power to act. And so, while it is true that the metal expands because it was heated, and that it has the power to expand and the liability to exercise that power when heated, the metal exists because God keeps it in being, and it has the power to expand and the liability to exercise that power when heated because God, a person, simultaneously sustains in it that power and liability in virtue of his basic powers. God thus keeps the laws of nature operative; and, in keeping in existence the material objects of our universe, he keeps operative the law of the conservation of matter. God also causes, claims theism, the existence of human persons and keeps them in existence from moment to moment; and he causes them to have and sustains in them their powers and beliefs. He does this in part by such means as sustaining in genes the powers to produce human beings, and in the molecules which form brains the powers to sustain human powers and beliefs. God also permits humans to form the purposes they do, but he does not make them choose this way rather than that. God thus provides a complete explanation of the universe and everything that happens in it, except in so far as he permits humans to make free choices. If the universe had a beginning, God created the first material objects then; if it has always existed, God by his action at each moment of everlasting time sustains material objects in existence always. Therefore, either way, he provides (in virtue of his continual choice to sustain material objects in existence), the ultimate explanation of the universe, except in so far as he permits humans to make free choices.

These three rivals for providing the ultimate explanation of all observable phenomena must be assessed by the four criteria for assessing proposed explanations which I analysed in Chapter 2. But when we are considering explanations of all observable phenomena, clearly, as we saw there, Criterion 3 drops out. When you are trying to explain everything observable, there are no neighbouring fields about which you can have knowledge, with which your theory needs to fit. So the application of the four criteria boils down to this. That theory of ultimate explanation is most likely to be the true one, which is the simplest theory that predicts the observable phenomena when we would not otherwise expect to find them. The thesis of this book is that theism provides by far the simplest explanation of all phenomena. Materialism is not, I shall argue, a simple hypothesis, and there is a range of phenomena which it is most unlikely ever to be able to explain. Humanism is an even less simple hypothesis than materialism.

As we shall see more fully in due course, the great complexity of materialism arises from this, that it postulates that any complete explanation of things behaving as they do is provided by the powers and liabilities of an immense (possibly infinite) number of material objects. Each of these is made of atoms, and the atoms are made of fundamental particles, such as electrons and protons; and some of these in their turn are made of quarks, and, for all we now know, the quarks are made of sub-quarks. These material objects belong to kinds, which have exactly the same powers and liabilities as each other. All bits of copper, as we have noted, have exactly the same powers to expand or melt or convey electricity, and the liabilities to exercise these powers under the same circumstances. For each event, there is a complete explanation of why it happened to be found in the powers and liabilities of the particular objects involved in it. There is a complete explanation of this stone falling to the ground in two seconds in the powers and liabilities of the stone and the earth (as codified by Newton's laws or whatever laws explain Newton's laws). And there is a complete explanation of this piece of copper expanding when heated in the powers and liabilities of this bit of copper.

If the universe had no beginning, **the ultimate explanation of how things are—according to the materialist**—therefore lies in the powers and liabilities of innumerable fundamental particles or of whatever material substances, such as chunks of matter-energy, brought the fundamental particles into existence. All of them, whether fundamental particles or chunks of matter-energy—by an enormous coincidence—have some of the same powers and liabilities as each other (e.g. all obeying the law of gravity); and they may fall into a few kinds (e.g. electrons or protons or their own more fundamental constituents). All members of each kind—by a further large coincidence—have their other powers and liabilities the same as each other. If the universe had a beginning, it began with material substances, probably forming a very condensed chunk of matter-energy, all of which (all parts of the condensed chunk) showed this general coincidence in their powers and liabilities.

Theism, I shall be arguing, can do a lot better. In this chapter I shall argue that theism is a very simple hypothesis, far simpler than the inanimate hypotheses which I have been analysing; and in subsequent chapters I shall show how theism leads us to expect to find the things which we do find—when we would not otherwise expect to find them.

The Simplicity of Theism

Theism claims that every other object which exists is caused to exist and kept in existence by just one substance, God. And it claims that every property which every substance has is due to God causing or permitting it to exist. It is a hallmark of a simple explanation to postulate few causes. There could in this respect be no simpler explanation than one which postulated **only one cause**. Theism is simpler than polytheism. And theism postulates for its one cause, a person, **infinite degrees of those properties which are essential to persons**—infinite power (God can do anything logically possible), infinite knowledge (God knows everything logically possible to know), and infinite freedom (no external cause influences which purposes God forms: God acts only in so far as he sees reason for acting.)

The hypothesis that there is an infinitely powerful, knowledgeable and free person is the hypothesis that there is a person with **zero limits** (apart from those of logic) to his power, knowledge, and freedom. Scientists have always seen postulating infinite degrees of some quantity as simpler than postulating some very large finite degree of that quantity, and have always done the former when it predicted observations equally well. Newton's theory of gravity postulated that the gravitational force travelled with infinite velocity, rather than with some very large finite velocity (say 2,000,000,000.325 km/sec.), which would have predicted the observations equally well within the limit of accuracy to which measurements could be made. Only when Einstein's General Theory of Relativity, concerned with electromagnetism as well as with gravity, was adopted as the simplest theory covering a vast range of data did scientists accept as a consequence of that theory that the gravitational force travelled with a finite velocity. Likewise in the Middle Ages people believed that light travelled with an infinite velocity rather than with some large finite velocity equally compatible with observations. Only when observations were made by Römer in the seventeenth century incompatible with the infinite-velocity theory was it accepted that light had a finite velocity.

Zero and infinity are opposites. To postulate that light travels with infinite velocity is to postulate that it takes zero time to reach any finitely distant destination. Scientists have shown a preference, similar to their preference for infinity, for theories which postulate zero degrees of some quantity rather than some very small degree of that quantity equally compatible with observations. They have preferred to postulate, for example, that photons (the particles of light) have zero rest mass (zero mass when stationary) rather than a very very small rest mass (say 2.62×10^{-1000} gms), when either hypothesis was equally compatible with anything which could have been observed.

Persons, as we have seen, are objects with (intentional) powers, purposes, and beliefs. If the action of a person is to explain the existence and operation of the universe, he will need to be a very powerful person. It is a simpler hypothesis to postulate that his power is infinite rather than just very large. If we said that he was powerful enough to make a universe of such and mass but not powerful enough to make a more massive one, the question would arise as to why there was just that rather than any other limit to his power. It naturally fits the suggestion that God's power is infinite that there be no causal influences influencing how he exercises that power, and so it is simplest to hold that his freedom too is infinite. In order to exercise power effectively, you need to know what are the consequences of your actions. Hence it naturally fits the claim that God is infinitely powerful and free to claim that he is infinitely knowledgeable. If we are to explain the various phenomena to be described in subsequent chapters by the purposive action of God, we shall need to suppose that he understands the consequences of his actions on a large scale. It is simplest to suppose that his understanding of things is unlimited. Hence the principles which we use in science and history and all other human enquiries into causes indicate that, if we are to explain the world in terms of personal explanation, we should postulate a personal being of infinite power, knowledge, and freedom.

It is simpler to suppose that God exists eternally. If he came into existence only at a certain past moment of time, there would have been some earlier period of time at which what happened would have had nothing to do with God. Other forces would have been at work, and it would have depended on them whether God came into being at all. And so our hypothesis postulated to explain how the world is would inevitably become more complicated, in postulating other forces and to that extent limited divine power. And the same applies if we supposed that God would cease to exist in future.

It seems to me that it is simpler to postulate not merely that God is eternally infinitely powerful, knowledgeable, and free, but that he is so essentially. If we were to say that it is only an accident that God is infinitely powerful, etc., we allow that God could, if he so chose, abdicate. He could reduce himself to a being of limited power. He could even commit suicide. And then it would be open to some rival to become infinitely powerful instead. But, in that case, it would have been an accident that our God was in charge of the universe; it could have been, and could yet happen, that another God took charge (maybe with less extensive powers.) But all of that would make it much less the foundational brute fact that our God is the source of all that is. It would need to be explained why God had not already limited his powers or committed suicide. And some other causal factors would be at work determining under what conditions some rival could become omnipotent. All that no longer requires explanation if we suppose that God is essentially omnipotent, omniscient, perfectly free, and eternal.

The motivation here is just the same as a similar motivation in physics which thinks of fundamental particles as the particles they are only if they retain their powers. The powers they have are part of what makes them the objects they are. An electron is an electron only if it repels all other electrons with a certain fixed force. At the bottom explanatory level, things are what they are partly in virtue of their powers.

A person could not be a person if he had zero degrees of power, knowledge, and freedom. To suppose a finite limit to these qualities is less simple than to suppose no limit. And to suppose infinite degrees of these qualities bound together, and bound to eternity, is to postulate the simplest kind of person there could be; and, as we saw in Chapter 1, all the other essential properties of God follow from the three properties of omnipotence, omniscience, and perfect freedom. Hence, theism provides the simplest kind of personal explanation of the universe there could be. God chooses for reasons, or between reasons, and brings about the universe because it is one of the many good things he could bring about.

God being omnipotent could bring about anything, and so showing that what we observe is to be expected if there is a God will consist in showing that what we observe belongs to a kind of universe that, in virtue of his perfect goodness, God has reason to bring about. That does not guarantee that he will bring it about, but it makes it quite likely. I shall show this for the range of phenomena we find around us, while at the same time showing the great complexity of any materialist explanation of some of these phenomena, and the inability of materialism to explain other phenomena at all.

4

HOW THE EXISTENCE OF GOD EXPLAINS THE WORLD AND ITS ORDER

The Universe and its Natural Laws

There is a physical universe consisting of innumerable differently sized chunks of matter. Our earth is one of several planets which travel around the sun, which is a small star, a big ball of flame. The star is one of many millions of stars in our galaxy, our group of stars, the Milky Way. Our galaxy belongs to a local cluster of galaxies, and astronomers can observe many thousands of millions of such clusters. Although very largely uniform, the universe contains much local 'clumping'. The stars and the planets are of different sizes, and planets such as our own are uneven in all sorts of ways—consider the differently sized and shaped pebbles on the sea shore.

It is extraordinary that there should exist anything at all. Surely the most natural state of affairs is simply nothing: no universe, no God, nothing. But there is something. And so many things. Maybe chance could have thrown up the odd electron. But so many particles! Not everything will have an explanation. But, as we have seen, the whole progress of science and **all** other **intellectual enquiry demands that**

we postulate the smallest number of brute facts. If we can explain the many bits of the universe by one simple being which keeps them in existence, we should do so—even if inevitably we cannot explain the existence of that simple being.

Yet not merely are there **enormous numbers of things**, but they **all behave** in certain respects **in exactly the same way**. The same laws of nature govern the most distant galaxies we can observe through our telescopes as operate on earth, and the same laws govern the earliest events in time to which we can infer as operate today. Or, as I prefer to put it, every object, however distant in time and space from ourselves, has in certain respects the same powers and the same liabilities to exercise those powers as do the particles of which our own bodies are made. If there is no cause of all this, it would be a most extraordinary coincidence—too extraordinary for any rational person to believe. But **science cannot explain why every object has the same powers and liabilities**. It can explain why an object has one power in virtue of it having some wider power (why this local law of nature operates in virtue of some more general law of nature operating). But it could not conceivably explain why each object has the most general powers it does. Suppose that Newton's three laws of motion and his law of gravitational attraction are the fundamental laws of nature. Then what that means is that every atom, every electron, and so on attracts every other object in the universe with exactly the same attractive force (i.e. one which varies with the square of their distance apart). Now Newtons's laws are not the fundamental laws of nature; they hold very accurately but not totally accurately, and only when the bodies with which they deal are not too massive and not moving too fast. But, to the extent to which Newton's laws do hold, that is because they follow from the laws of General Relativity and Quantum Theory; and maybe these are the consequences of some more general theory—Grand Unified Theory. But, wherever we stop, the same general point applies. Suppose we stop with Grand Unified Theory. Then every atom and every electron in the universe has just the same powers and liabilities—those described by Grand Unified Theory. And that, if you allow yourself only scientific explanations, is where you stop. That, says the materialist, is just how things are.

But that sort of stopping place is just where no rational enquirer will stop. If all the coins found on an archaeological site have the same markings, or all the documents in a room are written with the same characteristic handwriting, we look for an explanation in terms of a common source. The apparently coincidental cries out for explanation.

It is not merely that **all material objects** have the same very general powers and liabilities as each other (e.g. behaving in accord with Grand Unified Theory); but they **fall into kinds, members of which behave like each other in more specific ways.** Each electron behaves like each other electron in repelling every other electron with the same electrical force. There may be a scientific explanation of why particles of particular kinds have the powers and liabilities they do in terms of their being caused to exist by particles of some other kind. Thus protons are often caused to exist and have the powers and liabilities they do by the decay of neutrons (a neutron may decay into a proton, an electron, and a neutrino). But then an ultimate explanation of an inanimate kind would still be in terms of particles (or just chunks of matter-energy) of some few kinds which have the same powers and liabilities as each other. Larger objects fall into kinds, too. Oak trees behave like other oak trees, and tigers like other tigers. And many of these respects in which all material objects and objects of particular kinds behave like each other (for almost all the time) are also simple and so easily detectable by human beings. It might have happened that the ultimate constituents of matter (electrons, protons, photons, and suchlike, or whatever they are made of) behaved in the same simple ways, but that, when they came together to make medium-sized material objects, they behaved in such a complicated way that, from a mere superficial study of their behaviour, humans could never predict what would happen. Maybe one day rocks would fall apart, and on another day they would float in the air—but mere unscientific observation would not lead us to have the slightest idea which would happen when. But fortunately our world is not like that.

In our world there are **regularities in the behaviour of medium-sized objects** which can be readily detected and used by the unscientific—regularities which hold for almost all the time and to a high degree of approximation. Heavy objects fall to the ground, humans and other land animals need air to live, seeds planted and watered grow into plants, bread nourishes humans but grass does not. And so on. There are, of course, exceptions—there are cases when heavy objects will not fall to the ground (e.g. if they are heavily magnetized so as to be repelled by a magnet beneath them); and only a scientist can predict *exactly* how long an object will take to fall, and *exactly* how much bread humans need for normal activities. The obvious approximate regularities which humans can readily detect are ones **with important consequences for whether we live or die** (eat enough to live, escape predators and accidents), how we can mate, have children, keep warm, travel, and so on. By observing and understanding these regularities, humans can then utilize them to make a difference to the world outside our bodies, and thereby to our own lives. We need true beliefs about the effects of our basic actions if through them we are to make a difference to the world. But only if objects behave in regular ways sufficiently simple to be understood by humans will we be able to acquire those beliefs. By observing that bread nourishes, we can then take steps to stay alive by eating bread. By observing that seeds (including grains of wheat) when planted and watered grow into plants, we can then take steps to grow wheat to make into bread. And so on. But if material objects behaved totally erratically, we would never be able to choose to control the world or our own lives in any way. So, in seeking an explanation of why all material objects fall into a few kinds with the same simple powers and liabilities as each other, we should seek one which explains why these kinds are such that the approximate powers and liabilities of medium-sized material objects (including those of importance for human life) which follow therefrom are readily detectable by humans. For it is a pervasive feature of all material objects—that their powers and liabilities are such as to have this consequence.

The simple hypothesis of theism leads us to expect all the phenomena which I have been describing with some reasonable degree of

probability. God being omnipotent is able to produce a world orderly
in these respects. And he has good reason to choose to do so: a world
containing human persons is a good thing. Persons have experiences,
and thoughts, and can make choices, and their choices can make big
differences to themselves, to others, and to the inanimate world. And
humans have available to them a particular kind of free choice—the
freedom to choose between good and evil—which God himself does
not have and so will have very strong reason to bring about. God, being
perfectly good, is generous. With a body humans have a limited chunk
of matter under our control, and, if we so choose, we can choose to
learn how the world works and so learn which bodily actions will have
more remote effects. We can learn quickly when rocks are likely to fall,
predators to pounce, and plants to grow. Thereby God allows us to
share in his creative activity of choosing. We can make choices crucial
for ourselves—whether to avoid falling rocks, to escape from predators,
to plant crops in order to get enough to eat, or not to bother; whether
to build houses and live comfortably or to be content with a more
primitive life-style. And we can make choices crucial for other embodied
(and so publicly accessible) persons—whether to give them food or let
them starve.

But, because the approximate observable regularities in the behaviour
of medium-sized objects are due to more precise regularities in the
behaviour of their small-scale components, we can, if we so choose,
try to find out what are these latter components. With this knowledge
we can build instruments which extend further our knowledge and
control of the world. Humans can discover the laws of dynamics and
chemistry and so make cars and aeroplanes, or—alternatively—bombs
and guns; and so extend the range of our power from control merely of
our bodies and their local environment to a much wider control of the
world. Embodiment in an orderly world gives the possibility not merely
of quick learning of regularities utilizable for survival, but of science and
technology—of discovering by co-operative effort over the years deep
laws which can be utilized to rebuild our world in the ways we choose. It
is up to us whether we choose to learn and extend control, and up to us

how we extend control. Like a good parent, a generous God has reason for not foisting on us a certain fixed measure of knowledge and control, but rather for giving us a choice of whether to grow in knowledge and control.

It is because it provides these opportunities for humans that God has a reason to create a world governed by natural laws of the kind we find. Of course God has reason to make many other things, and I would hesitate to say that one could be certain that he would make such a world. But clearly it is the sort of thing that there is some significant probability that he will make.

The suitability of the world as a theatre for **humans is not the only reason for God to make an orderly world**. The higher animals too are conscious, learn, and plan—and the predictability of things in their most easily detectable aspects enables them to do so. But beyond that an orderly world is a beautiful world. Beauty consists in patterns of order. Total chaos is ugly. The movements of the stars in accord with regular laws is a beautiful dance. The medievals thought of the planets as carried by spheres through the sky, and their regular movements producing the 'music of the spheres' whose beauty humans casually ignored, although it was one of the most beautiful things there is. God has reason to make an orderly world, because beauty is a good thing—in my view whether or not anyone ever observes it, but certainly if only one person ever observes it.

The argument to God from the world and its regularity is, I believe, a codification by philosophers of a natural and rational reaction to an orderly world deeply embedded in the human consciousness. Humans see the comprehensibility of the world as evidence of a comprehending creator. The prophet Jeremiah lived in an age in which the existence of a creator-god of some sort was taken for granted. What was at stake was the extent of his goodness, knowledge, and power. Jeremiah argued from the order of the world that he was a powerful and reliable god, that god was the sort of God that I described in Chapter 1. Jeremiah argued to the power of the creator from the extent of the creation-'The host of heaven cannot be numbered, neither the sand of the sea measured' (Jer. 33: 22); and he argued that its regular behaviour showed the reliability of the creator, and he spoke of the 'covenant of the day and night' whereby they follow each other regularly, and 'the ordinances of heaven and earth' (Jer. 33: 20–1 and 25–6).

The orderly behaviour of material bodies, which he describes as their tendency to move towards a goal (e.g. the falling body tending towards the ground, the air bubbling up through water), was the basis of the fifth of St Thomas Aquinas's 'five ways' to prove the existence of God:

> The fifth way is based on the guidedness of things. For we see that certain things lacking awareness, viz, natural bodies, move so as to attain a goal. This is evident from the fact that always or very frequently they behave in the same way and there follows the best result—which shows that they truly tend to a goal, and do not merely hit it by accident. Nothing however that lacks awareness tends to a goal, except under the direction of someone with awareness and with understanding; the arrow, for example, requires an archer. Everything in nature, therefore, is directed to its goal by someone with understanding and this we call 'God'.
>
> (*Summa Theologiae* Ia 2.3)

The argument from the existence and regular behaviour of material objects to a God who keeps them in existence with the same powers and liabilities as each other is an argument which satisfies very well the criteria set out in Chapter 2. The hypothesis of theism is a simple hypothesis which leads us to expect these observable phenomena, when no other simple hypothesis will do so. The perfect goodness of God follows from his three simple properties of being essentially omnipotent, omniscient and perfectly free. It follows from his goodness that he is likely to produce humans, and it is necessary for our survival that we live in a universe with the sort of regularity we find. On the materialist hypothesis it is a mere coincidence that material objects have the same powers as each other, and not a simple stopping point for explanation. Because theism satisfies the criteria so well, the existence and regular behaviour of material objects provide good evidence for the existence of God.

Human and Animal Bodies

The orderliness of nature in the regular behaviour of objects over time, codified in natural laws, is not the only facet of the orderliness of the natural world. There is also **the marvellous order of human and animal bodies.** They are like very very complicated machines. They have delicate sense organs which are sensitive to so many aspects of the environment, and cause us to have true beliefs about our environment. We learn where the objects around us are, where our friends are and where our enemies are, where there is food and where there is poison—through our eyes turning light rays and our ears turning sound waves into nerve impulses. And by using these resultant beliefs we can move ourselves, our arms and hands and mouths—to climb and hold rocks and talk—as basic actions in ways which enable us to achieve all sorts of diverse goals (including those needed for our survival). The complex and intricate organization of human and animal bodies, which made them effective vehicles for us to acquire knowledge and perform actions in these ways, was something which struck the anatomists and naturalists of the eighteenth century even more than those of earlier centuries (partly because the invention of the microscope at the end of the seventeenth century allowed them to see just how intricately organized those bodies were).

Very many eighteenth-century writers argued that there was no reason to suppose that chance would throw up such beautiful organization, whereas God was able to do so and had abundant reason to do so—in the goodness, to which I have drawn attention in my own way earlier in the chapter, of the existence of embodied animals and humans. Hence their existence, they argued, was good evidence of the existence of God. I believe this argument (as so far stated) to be correct, by the criteria given in Chapter 2. As I argued earlier, God has reason for creating embodied persons and animals, and so for creating human and animal bodies. God is able to bring about the existence of such bodies. That he does so, we saw in Chapter 3, is a simple hypothesis. Hence there is good reason to believe that God is the creator of human and animal bodies. Their existence provides another strand of evidence (additional to that provided by the existence of the universe and its conformity to natural laws) for the existence of God.

The best-known presentation of this argument was by **William Paley** in his *Natural Theology* (1806), which begins with the famous passage:

In crossing a heath, suppose I pitched my foot against a *stone*, and were asked how the stone came to be there, I might possibly answer, that, for anything I knew to the contrary, it had lain there for ever; nor would it, perhaps, be very easy to show the absurdity of this answer. But suppose I had found a *watch* upon the ground, and it should be inquired how the watch happened to be in that place, I should hardly think of the answer which I had before given—that, for anything I knew, the watch might have always been there. Yet why should not this answer serve for the watch as well as for the stone? Why is it not as admissible in the second case as in the first? For this reason, and for no other, viz., that, when we come to inspect the watch, we perceive (what we could not discover in the stone) that its several parts are framed and put together for a purpose, e.g., that they are so formed and adjusted as to produce motion, and that motion so regulated as to point out the hour of the day; that, if the different parts had been differently shaped from what they are, of a different size from what they are, or placed after any other manner, or in any other order than that in which they are placed, either no motion at all would have been carried on in the machine, or none which would have answered the use that is now served by it . . . The inference, we think, is inevitable, that the watch must have had a maker: that there must have existed, at some time, and at some place or other, an artificer or artificers who formed it for the purpose which we find it actually to answer; who comprehended its construction, and designed its use.

The rest of Paley's book is devoted to showing how well built in all their intricate detail are animals and humans, and so to concluding that they must have had God as their maker. This analogy of animals to complex machines seems to me correct, and its conclusion justified.

The argument does **not**, however, give **any reason to suppose that God made humans and animals** as a basic act **on one particular day** in history, rather than through a gradual process. And, as we now know, humans and animals did come into existence through the gradual process of evolution from a primitive soup of matter which formed as earth cooled down some 4,000 million years ago. In that process natural selection played a central role. Darwin's *Origin of Species* (1859) taught us the outlines of the story, and biologists have been filling in the details ever since. The clear simple modern presentation in Richard Dawkins's *The Blind Watchmaker* (1986) is deservedly popular.

Because the story is so well known, I shall summarize it in a quick and very condensed paragraph. Molecules of the primitive soup combined by chance into a very simple form of life which reproduced itself. It produced offspring very similar to itself but each of them differing slightly by chance in various respects. In virtue of these differences, some of the offspring were better adapted to survive and so survived; others were not well equipped to survive and did not survive. The next generations of offspring produced on average the characteristics of their parents, but exhibited slight variations from them in various ways. The more a characteristic gave an advantage in the struggle for survival, the more evolution favoured its development. Other things being equal, complexity of organization was a characteristic with survival value, and so more complex organisms began to appear on earth. A characteristic which gave an advantage to complex organisms was sexual reproduction, and so gradually today's male and female organisms evolved. Whatever characteristic of an animal you name, there is a story to be told of how it came to have that characteristic in terms of it being one of many characteristics which were slight variants on the characteristics of parents, and it giving an advantage in the struggle for survival over the other characteristics. Once upon a time giraffes had necks of the same length as other animals of their bodily size. But by chance some giraffe couples produced offspring with longer necks than usual. These offspring with the longer necks were better able to reach food (e.g. leaves in the tree tops) than the others, and so they flourished and more of them survived to have more offspring than did those with shorter necks. The offspring of the longer-necked giraffes had on average necks of the same lengths as their own parents, but some had ones slightly longer and others had ones slightly shorter. There was an advantage in even longer necks, and so the average neck of the population became longer. But giraffes with very long necks proved less able to escape from predators—they could not escape from woods or run so fast when pursued by lions. So the length of giraffe necks stabilized at an optimum size—long enough for giraffes to get the leaves but not so long as to make them unable to escape from predators. That, or something like it, is the explanation of why the giraffe has a long neck. And there is a similar story to be told for every animal and human characteristic. A little sensitivity to light gave some advantage (to many animals in many environments) in the struggle for survival, a little more sensitivity gave more advantage, and hence the eye developed in many animals. And, above all, complexity of nervous organization in supporting a range of sense organs and bodily movements gave great advantage, and so we have the complexly organized animals and humans we have today.

So, in summary, **the Darwinian explanation** of why there are the complex animal and human bodies there are today is that once upon a time there were certain chemicals on earth, and, given the laws of evolution (e.g. reproduction with slight variation), it was probable that complex organisms would emerge. This explanation of the existence of complex organisms is surely a full explanation, but it **is not an ultimate explanation** of that fact. For an ultimate explanation we need an explanation at the highest level of why those laws rather than any other ones operated, and why there were those chemicals on earth. The laws of evolution are no doubt consequences of laws of chemistry governing the organic matter of which animals are made. And the laws of chemistry hold because the fundamental laws of physics hold. But why just those fundamental laws of physics rather than any others? If the laws of physics did not have the consequence that some chemical arrangement would give rise to life, or that there would be random variations by offspring from characteristics of parents, and so on, there would be no evolution by natural selection. So, even given that there are laws of nature (i.e. that material objects have the same powers and liabilities as each other), why just those laws?

Recent scientific work has drawn attention to the fact that if the laws of nature are of the same kind as our actual laws, the constants of those laws have to lie within very narrow bands indeed if life was to evolve anywhere in the universe. If several of the constants had a value greater or less than their actual value by one part in a million, no animal life, let alone human life, would have evolved. By 'laws of the same kind as our actual laws', I mean laws of the four forces which physicists have analysed—gravity, electromagnetism, the strong nuclear force, and the weak force. By the 'constants' of laws of nature I mean those fixed numerical values which determine how forces are determined by the masses, electric charges, distances apart etc. of bodies. Thus the law of gravity states that $F = G \frac{mm^1}{r^2}$; this means that the force of gravity whereby two bodies attract each other is G times the product of their masses (m and m^1 respectively) and inversely proportional to the square of their distance apart (r). (For a very short simple account of this **'fine tuning'** see John Leslie *Universes,* pages 2–6; and for a fuller and somewhat more recent account see Paul Davies, *The Goldilocks Enigma*, chapters 1–7, especially chapter 7.)

The materialist says that there is no explanation why there are just the laws there are. The theist claims that God has a reason for bringing about those laws because those laws have the consequence that eventually animals and humans evolve.

Even given that the laws of physics are such as to give rise to laws of evolution of complex organisms from a certain primitive soup of matter, animals and humans will evolve only if there is a primitive soup with the right chemical constitution to start with. Some soups different in chemical constitution from that from which the earth actually began would also, given the actual laws of physics, have given rise to animals. But most soups of chemical elements made from differently arranged fundamental particles would not have given rise to animals. So why was there that particular primitive soup? We can trace the history of the world further backwards. The primitive soup existed because the earth was formed in the way it was; and the earth was formed in the way it was because the galaxy was formed in the way it was, and so on . . . until we come right back to the **Big Bang**, the explosion 13,500 million years ago with which apparently the universe began. The matter-energy at the time of the Big Bang had to have a density and a velocity of recession, again within very narrow bands, if it was to bring forth life. For example, if the Big Bang had caused the chunks of matter-energy to recede from each other a little more quickly, no galaxies, stars, or planets, and no environment suitable for life, would have been formed on earth or anywhere else in the universe. If the recession had been marginally slower, the universe would have collapsed in on itself before life could have been formed. If there is an ultimate scientific explanation, it will have to leave it as a brute fact that the universe began in such a state and had such natural laws as to be life evolving, when a marginal difference in those initial conditions would have ensured that no life ever evolved anywhere.

Of course, **the universe** may not have had a beginning with a Big Bang, but **may have lasted forever**. Even so, its matter must have had certain general features if at any time there was to be a state of the universe suited to produce animals and humans. There would need, for example, to be enough matter but not too much of it for chemical substances to be built up at some time or other—a lot of fundamental particles are needed but with large spaces between them. And it remains the case that only a certain narrow range of laws would allow there to be animals and humans at any time ever. Again the materialist will have to leave it as an ultimate brute fact that an everlasting universe and its laws had those characteristics, whereas the theist has a simple ultimate explanation of why things are thus: that by his action at each moment of everlasting time God keeps them thus. He has reason to do this, among other reasons, in order to ensure that humans will evolve at some time on earth (and maybe also at other times on other planets).

True, God could have created humans without doing so by the long process of evolution. But that is only an objection to the theistic hypothesis if you suppose that God's only reason for creating anything is for the sake of human beings. To repeat my earlier point—God also has reason to bring about animals. Animals are conscious beings who enjoy much life and perform intentional actions, even if they do not choose freely which ones to do. Of course God has a reason for giving life to elephants and giraffes, tigers and snails. And anyway, the beauty of the evolution of the inanimate world from the Big Bang (or from eternity) would be quite enough of a reason for producing it, even if God were the only person to have observed it. But he is not; we ourselves can now admire earlier and earlier stages of cosmic evolution through our telescopes. God paints with a big brush from a large paintbox and he has no need to be stingy with the paint he uses to paint a beautiful universe.

Darwin showed that the universe is a machine for making animals and humans. But it is misleading to gloss that correct point in the way that Richard Dawkins does: 'our own existence once presented the greatest of all mysteries, but . . . it is a mystery no longer . . . Darwin and Wallace solved it' (*The Blind Watchmaker*, p. xiii). It is misleading because it ignores the interesting question of whether the existence and operation of that machine, the factors which Darwin (and Wallace) cited to explain 'our own existence', themselves have a further explanation. I have argued that the principles of rational enquiry suggest that they do. Darwin gave a full explanation of the existence of animals and humans; but not, I think, a complete or ultimate one. The watch may have been made with the aid of some blind screwdrivers (or even a blind watchmaking machine), but they were guided by a watchmaker with some very clear sight.

An objector may invoke a form of what is known as the **anthropic principle** to urge that, unless the universe exhibited order of the kinds which I have described (simple laws operating on matter in such a way as to lead to the evolution of animals and humans), there would not be any humans alive to comment on the fact. Hence there is nothing surprising in the fact that we find evolving order—we could not possibly find anything else. This argument, however, fails totally for a reason which can best be brought out by an analogy. Suppose that a madman kidnaps a victim and shuts him in a room with a card-shuffling machine. The machine shuffles ten packs of cards simultaneously and then draws a card from each pack and exhibits simultaneously the ten cards. The kidnapper tells the victim that he will shortly set the machine to work and it will exhibit its first draw, but that, unless the draw consists of an ace of hearts from each pack, the machine will simultaneously set off an explosion that will kill the victim, in consequence of which he will not see which cards the machine drew. The machine is then set to work, and to the amazement and relief of the victim the machine exhibits an ace of hearts drawn from each pack. The victim thinks that this extraordinary fact needs an explanation in terms of the machine having been rigged in some way. But the kidnapper, who now reappears, casts doubt on this suggestion. 'It is hardly surprising', he says, 'that the machine draws only aces of hearts. You could not possibly see anything else. For you would not be here to see anything at all, if any other cards had been drawn.' But, of course, the victim is right and the kidnapper is wrong. There is indeed something extraordinary in need of explanation in ten aces of hearts being drawn. The fact that this peculiar order is a necessary condition of the draw being perceived at all makes what is perceived no less extraordinary and in need of explanation. The theist's starting-point is not that we perceive order rather than disorder, but that order rather than disorder is there. Maybe only if order is there can we know what is there, but that makes what is there no less extraordinary and in need of explanation. True, every draw, every arrangement of matter, is equally improbable a priori—that is, if chance alone dictates what is drawn. But if a person is arranging things, he has reason to produce some arrangements rather than others (ten aces of hearts, a world fine-tuned to produce animals and humans). And if we find such arrangements, that is reason for supposing that a person is doing the arranging.

Another objector may advocate what is called the many-worlds theory. He may say that if there are trillions and trillions of universes (what is called a **'multiverse'**) exhibiting between them many very different kinds of order and disorder, it is very probable that one of these universes will be governed by simple comprehensible laws which are (human and animal) life-evolving. But we need a reason to suppose there are any universes other than our own. The only reason we could have is that a theory of physics, which is probable on the evidence we can observe in our universe (probable by the criteria set out in Chapter 2), has the consequence that universes (or just a single energy field) 'give birth' to other universes which differ from each other in their laws and initial conditions (that is, the way in which matter-energy was arranged at their beginning). (For description of the kinds of multiverse which recent physicists have postulated, see Paul Davies, *The Goldilocks Enigma*, chapter 9.) From that it would follow that our universe was born from an older universe (or field) and may give birth to one or more younger universes, these universes differing from ours in their laws and initial conditions. Most of these universes, unlike our universe, would not have laws and initial conditions which give rise to animals and humans. But this whole system of universes, this multiverse, would itself be governed by laws and would itself have had certain initial conditions, or (if it did not have a beginning) other general features, which had the consequence that at some time or other it would produce a universe, which is (human and animal) life-evolving (that is, would produce animals and humans on some planet or other). This multiverse would thus have very general laws which would take more specific forms in each universe, and would in our universe take the form of life-evolving laws. The multiverse would thus itself be life-evolving. All this is what would need to be shown by the advocate of many-worlds, before we can take this suggestion seriously.

But if we do take it seriously, the argument from the operation of natural laws will proceed as before. The fact that the multiverse is governed by very general laws, simple enough for us to comprehend (as they must be if we are to be justified in postulating a multiverse), means that **all the material objects throughout the multiverse have the same very general simple powers and liabilities as each other**. We should try to find an explanation of this very striking fact; and we have the same reason as before for postulating God as that explanation (by the criteria of Chapter 2).

Further we must note that instead of the actual multiverse (to which our universe belongs) there could have been a different multiverse (itself governed by laws of quite different kinds, and having quite different initial conditions or other general features) such that at no time would it give birth to a universe which was life-evolving. And **innumerable different possible multiverses** would be like this, **not-life-evolving**. So if we find reason to suppose that our universe does belong to a multiverse, we should try to find an explanation of why that actual multiverse is life-evolving; that is, why its very general laws and initial conditions (or other general features) are such as at some time to lead to the evolution of a universe which would at some time give rise to humans and animals. And again we have the same reason as before for postulating that God brought this about. God is a simple being (far simpler than a multiverse) who may be expected to bring about the existence of humans and animals and so a universe containing them, and so to ensure that if he brings about a multiverse, it is life-evolving; otherwise there is no reason to suppose that a multiverse would be life-evolving.

Possible multiverses are of different sizes; some would contain only one universe, others would contain an infinity of universes. They are also of different kinds. What I shall call **'narrow' multiverses** would contain only universes having a similar kind of matter to our universe governed by laws of the same form as our laws (laws of gravitation, electromagnetism, and the other two forces) but containing different constants. (The constants in laws of nature determine the strength of forces. So the forces of gravity and electromagnetism in such universes might be either stronger or weaker than ours.) Many physicists believe a version of what is called 'inflation theory', which postulates that we belong to a multiverse of this kind. But what I shall call **'wide' possible multiverses** would contain universes having different kinds of matter from each other governed by laws of different forms from each other and from those which operate in our universe. A wide multiverse might for example include a universe with laws for twelve different kinds of force acting between bodies, the strength of which varies with the quantity of certain properties possessed by each body, these properties being of kinds which are not found in our universe (properties quite different from the mass, electric charge, etc. of bodies which determine their behaviour in our universe). The wider the multiverse (that is, the more universes of very different kinds it contains), the more probable it would be that it would include a universe which is life-evolving. So it might seem that if there exists *any very wide multiverse*, it would be quite probable that it would contain humans. But **the very general laws of a very wide multiverse of this kind would have to be enormously complicated**. Any very general laws, by which some parent universe would produce daughter universes governed by quite different kinds of specific laws from those which operated in the parent universe, would need to be far more complicated than ones which merely produced universes governed by laws differing from the laws of the parent universe only by containing different constants. (To take an analogy, a machine which produces chocolates and other sweets of different kinds has to be more complicated than one which merely produces bars of chocolate of the same kind but of different sizes.) That means that a theory of physics which postulated (on the basis of evidence observable in our universe) a narrower and so simpler multiverse would always satisfy criterion (2) (on page 24) better than one which postulated a wider multiverse. So we would need a lot of new observational evidence (more than we are ever likely to obtain merely by observing our universe, which is all we can do) which couldn't be explained by supposing that we belonged only to a narrow multiverse, before we would be justified in postulating a wide multiverse. And even if *every* wide multiverse would be life-evolving, the question would still remain why there is a wide multiverse rather than a narrow multiverse or just one universe (rather than no universe at all.)

But if there was a very wide multiverse, not merely is it probable that it would contain a universe like ours, but it is probable that it would contain also many other universes containing humans. Yet **most of these other universes containing humans would be unlike ours in many respects**. The laws which govern many such universes might only have simple enough consequences for their few human inhabitants to make predictions and use them to guide their behaviour in a small region. The humans who lived there might have no power to influence themselves or each other for good or ill. They might live in hard shells, unable to hurt or benefit each other. Food might be abundant, and there might be no need of co-operation in order to produce food. Babies might come into existence in an asexual way without the need for parental care. Humans might have no natural love for each other and no sense of morality. And there might be kinds of suffering far worse than those which exist in our universe. The fact that we find ourselves in a universe which is not like that, but is one where we can live greatly worthwhile lives (the features mentioned on pages 48–9) and can come to understand how things behave trillions of miles away, is to be expected (by the criteria of Chapter 2) if God brought about our universe (possibly as a member of a narrow multiverse), but far less probable if there was a vast wide multiverse not caused by God. By criterion (4) the fact that we find ourselves in a universe which has the features of our universe which I have just mentioned is far more to be expected if our universe (or a narrow multiverse to which it belongs) was created by God than if it is just a member of a vast wide multiverse not created by God. The rational enquirer must go on the evidence available, and even if it leads to a multiverse, it will most likely be a relatively narrow multiverse, and there being such a multiverse makes no difference to the argument of this chapter.

So there is our universe (or multiverse). It is characterized by vast, all-pervasive temporal order, the conformity of nature to formula, recorded in the scientific laws formulated by humans. It started off in such a way (or through eternity has been characterized by such features) as to lead to the evolution of animals and humans. **These phenomena are clearly things 'too big' for science to explain**. They are where science stops. They constitute the framework of science itself. I have argued that it is not a rational conclusion to suppose that explanation stops where science does, and so we should look for a personal explanation of the existence, conformity to law, and evolutionary potential of the universe. **Theism provides** just such **an explanation**. That is strong grounds for believing it to be true—by the criteria which I set out in Chapter 2. Note that I am not postulating a 'God of the gaps', a god merely to explain the things which science has not yet explained. I am postulating a God to explain what science explains; I do not deny that science explains, but I postulate God to explain why science explains. The very success of science in showing us how deeply orderly the natural world is provides strong grounds for believing that there is an even deeper cause of that order.

5

HOW THE EXISTENCE
OF GOD EXPLAINS
THE EXISTENCE
OF HUMANS

In writing loosely in the last chapter of evolutionary processes causing the existence of animals and humans, I glossed over something all important. Evolutionary processes certainly cause the existence of animal and human bodies in virtue of the laws of nature discovered by the physical sciences (sustained, I claim, by God). But there is more to humans than their bodies. **Humans (and the higher animals) are conscious beings**. They have thoughts and feelings; atoms do not have thoughts and feelings. But consciousness, I shall be arguing, cannot be the property of a mere body, a material object. It must be a property of something else connected to a body; and to that something else I shall give the traditional name of soul. At some time in evolutionary history bodies of complex animals became connected to souls, and this, I shall be arguing, is something utterly beyond the power of science to explain. But theism can explain this—for God has the power and reason to join souls to bodies. First, however, I need to describe the phenomena, and to bring out that humans (and the higher animals) consist of two parts—a body which is a material substance, and a soul which is an immaterial substance and to which the conscious life of thought and feeling belongs. I shall make my case with respect to humans, and then point out briefly that the same holds for the higher animals.

Human Souls

The world, I pointed out in Chapter 2, consists of substances. Tables and chairs, persons, nerve cells and bones are all substances. Substances have properties such as being brown or square, and relations to other substances such as being 10 feet away from another desk or coming into existence after it. A particular substance having a particular property or relation at a particular time is an event—for example, my tie being green at 8 a.m. on 1 January 1995, or a certain neurone (a nerve cell) firing (i.e. quickly discharging electricity) at 2 p.m. on 2 January 1994. Anything is a substance if it can cause an event, or if something can cause a change in it. So, as well as material substances, substances which occupy volumes of space, there may be immaterial ones as well, which do not occupy space. I am arguing in this book that there is a God who is such an immaterial substance; and, if there are ghosts and poltergeists, they too are immaterial substances. I am going to argue in this chapter that the essential part of each one of us is a soul which is an immaterial substance.

The history of the world is just the sequence of all the events which have ever happened. If you knew all the events which had happened (which substances existed, which properties and relations they had to which other substances when), you would know all that had ever happened.

Properties and events may be physical or mental. I shall understand by a **physical** event one such that no one person is necessarily better placed to know that it has happened than is any other person. Physical events are public; there is no privileged access to them. Thus my desk being square is a physical event because, even though I may be the only person to have observed this, anyone else could check that it is square just as well as I can. Among physical events are brain events. Whether a certain neurone in the brain fired at a particular time is something which could be observed equally well by many different observers, and so the firing is also a physical event. **Mental events**, by contrast, are ones which just one person has a special way of finding out about—by actually experiencing them. The person whose events these are has privileged access to them, a means of finding out about them which no one else can share.

Evidently—more evidently than anything else—there really are mental events, as we know from our own experience. They include patterns of colour in one's visual field, pains and thrills, beliefs, thoughts, and feelings. They also include the purposes which I try to realize through my body or in some other way, which I discussed in Chapter 2. My being in pain at midday yesterday, or having a red image in my visual field, or thinking about lunch, or forming the purpose of going to London, are such that if others could find out about them by some method, I could find out about them by the same method. Others can learn about my pains and thoughts by studying my behaviour and perhaps also by studying my brain. Yet I, too, could study my behaviour: I could watch a film of myself; I could study my brain—via a system of mirrors and microscopes—just as well as anyone else could. But, of course, I have a way of knowing about pains, thoughts, and suchlike other than those available to the best other student of my behaviour or brain: I actually experience them. Consequently, they must be distinct from brain events, or any other bodily events. A neurophysiologist cannot observe the quality of the colour in my visual field, or the pungency of the smell of roast beef which I smell. A Martian who came to earth, captured a human being, and inspected his brain could discover everything that was happening in that brain but would still wonder 'Does this human really feel anything when I stamp on his toe?' It is a further fact beyond the occurrence of brain events that there are pains and after-images, thoughts, and intentions. Likewise, such events are to be distinguished from the behaviour to which they typically give rise. People have sensations to which they give no expression—pains which they conceal or dream sensations which they report to no one—and, if the sensations give rise to behaviour, the subject is aware of the sensation as a separate event from the behaviour to which it gives rise.

I emphasize my definition of the mental as that to which the subject has privileged access. There are many properties which we attribute to people, which we might sometimes call 'mental' but which are not mental in my sense but are merely properties of public behaviour. When we say that someone is generous or irritable or a useful source of information, it may be that we are just saying something about the way they behave in public, not anything about the life of thought and feeling which lies behind such behaviour. We may naturally describe being irritable as a mental property, but it is not a mental property in my defined sense. My concern is to make the point that there are mental events in my sense, distinct from brain events. In making this point, I do not for one moment wish to deny that most of my mental events are caused by my brain events. An event in my brain (itself caused by an event in my tooth) caused my toothache; and another event in my brain (itself caused by the branch outside the window moving) caused my belief that the branch moved. But the point is that, just as ignition of petrol is distinct from the explosion which it subsequently causes, so the brain event is distinct from the pain or whatever else, which it causes. And, of course, there is causation in the other direction too: my purposes cause (unintentionally) the brain events which in turn cause the motion of my limbs (which I intend).

Humans, unlike inanimate things, have mental properties; they have a mental life. But there is more to humans than just having a mental life connected to a body. That **mental life** itself, I now argue, **is the state of an immaterial substance, a soul**, which is connected to the body. That humans consist of two connected substances—body and soul—is the view known as substance dualism. The alternative is to say that humans are just bodies (I am the same thing as that which we loosely call my body). In that case, my mental properties, such as being in pain or having an after-image, would be properties of my body. Let us call this view about humans *substance monism*—the view that there are only substances of one kind, material substances. If monism were correct, then there would be nothing more to the history of the world than the succession of those events which involve material substances, their coming into existence or ceasing to exist, and having properties and relations (physical or mental). But, I am now going to point out, if you knew all that, you would still not know one of the most important things of all—whether you or any other human continued over time to live a conscious life.

Let me illustrate this with the example of **brain transplants**. The brain consists of two hemispheres and a brain-stem. There is good evidence that humans can survive and behave as conscious beings if much of one hemisphere is destroyed. Now imagine my brain (hemispheres plus brain-stem) divided into two, and each half-brain taken out of my skull and transplanted into the empty skull of a body from which a brain has just been removed; and there to be added to each half-brain from some other brain (e.g. the brain of my identical twin) whatever other parts (e.g. more brain-stem) are necessary in order for the transplant to take and for there to be two living persons with lives of conscious experiences. Now I am very well aware that an operation of this delicacy is not at present practically possible and perhaps never will be possible for mere human scientists with mere human resources; but I cannot see that there are any insuperable theoretical difficulties standing in the way of such an operation. (Indeed that is a mild understatement—I fully expect it to be done one day.) We are, therefore, entitled to ask the further question—if this operation were done and we then had two living persons, both with lives of conscious experiences, which would be me? Probably both would to some extent behave like me and claim to be me and to remember having done what I did; for behaviour and speech depend, in large part, on brain-states, and there are very considerable overlaps between the 'information' carried by the two hemispheres which gives rise to behaviour and speech. But both persons would not be me. For if they were both identical with me, they would be the same person as each other (if *a* is the same as *b*, and *b* is the same as *c*, then *a* is the same as *c*) and they are not. They now have different experiences and lead different lives. There remain three other possibilities: that the person with my right half-brain is me, or that the person with my left half-brain is me, or that neither is me. But we cannot be certain which holds. It follows that mere knowledge of what happens to brains or bodies or anything else material does not tell you what happens to persons.

It is tempting to say that it is a matter of arbitrary definition which of the three possibilities is correct. But this temptation must be resisted. There is **a crucial factual issue here**—which can be shown if we imagine that I have been captured by a mad surgeon who is about to perform the split-brain operation on me. He tells me (and I have every reason to believe him) that the person to be formed from my left half-brain is to have an enjoyable life and the person to be formed from my right half-brain is to be subjected to a life of torture. Whether my future life will be happy or very painful, or whether I shall survive an operation at all, are clearly factual questions. (Only someone under the grip of some very strong philosophical dogma would deny that.) Yet, as I await the transplant and know exactly what will happen to my brain, I am in no position to know the answer to the question—what will happen to me. Maybe neither future person will be me—it may be that cutting the brain-stem will destroy the original person once and for all, and that, although repairing the severed stem will create two new persons, neither of them will be me. Perhaps I will be the left half-brain person, or maybe it will be the right half-brain person who will be me. Even if one subsequent person resembles the earlier me more in character and memory claims than does the other, that one may not be me. Maybe I will survive the operation but be changed in character and have lost much of my memory as a result of it, in consequence of which the other subsequent person will resemble the earlier me more in his public behaviour than I will.

Reflection on this thought experiment shows that, **however much we know about what has happened to my brain**—we may know exactly what has happened to every atom in it—and to every other material part of me, **we do not necessarily know what has happened to me**. From that it follows that there must be more to me than the matter of which my body and brain are made, a further essential immaterial part whose continuing in existence makes the brain (and so body) to which it is connected my brain (and body), and to this something I give the traditional name of 'soul'. I am my soul plus whatever brain (and body) it is connected to. Normally my soul goes when my brain goes, but in unusual circumstances (such as when my brain is split) it is uncertain where it goes.

Take a slightly different example. I die of a brain haemorrhage which today's doctors cannot cure, but my relatives take my corpse and put it straight into a deep freeze in California. Shortly thereafter there is an earthquake as a result of which my frozen brain is split into many parts, a few of which get lost. However, fifty years later, when medical technology has improved, my descendants take the bits of my broken corpse, warm it up and mend it, replacing the missing parts from elsewhere. The body becomes the body of a living person who behaves somewhat like me and seems to remember quite a lot of my past life. Have I come to life again, or not? Maybe, maybe not. Again there is a truth here, about whether I have survived the haemorrhage as I wanted to, and yet a truth of which we cannot be sure, however much we know about the story of my brain. Hence, my survival consists in the continuing of something else, which I call my soul, linked to my previous body; and I survive in this new body if and only if that soul is connected with it. And note that the extra truth is not a truth about what kind of mental life is connected to the brain. It is not a truth about mental properties, about what thoughts and feelings and purposes the revived person has. Rather, **the extra truth**, the truth about whether I have survived, **is a truth about who—that is, which substance—those properties are instantiated in**. And, since mere knowledge of what has happened to every material substance does not tell me that, it must be a truth about an immaterial substance. So long as I continue to have thoughts and feelings and purposes, I have survived any operation—whatever happens to any material parts of me. So my soul is the essential part of me—its survival constitutes my survival; and thoughts, feelings, and so on belong to me in virtue of belonging to my soul. The soul is the essential part of the human person.

Dualism is not a popular philosophical position today, but I find these arguments (of an entirely non-theological kind) in its favour inescapable. You have left something all-important out of the history of the world if you tell just the story of which physical events were succeeded by which other physical events. How people thought and felt is all-important. And equally important is who had those thoughts and feelings—when did one person cease to exist and another come into being.

Now certainly, as I have written, we normally know the answers to these questions. I do not wish to question any of our common-sense judgements about when someone is conscious, and who that person is. Our observation of bodies normally tells us when persons are the same and what they are feeling. Of course, if a baby screams when prodded with a needle, it is in pain. But it is not so obvious, when a human-looking organism made in a factory or a creature from another planet is prodded with a needle and emits some sound, whether that is in pain. And, of course, the person with this body today who has not been subject to a brain operation and shares the same patterns of behaviour as the person with this body yesterday is the same person as the latter. But after humans, let alone creatures from some distant planet, have had massive brain operations, it is not at all clear whether we are dealing with the same person as before. What these examples bring out is that someone feeling pain is a different event from their being prodded by a needle, and this person being the same person as that is different from this body being the same body as that; even if normally an event of the latter kind goes with an event of the former kind. **A full history of the world will tell the story of feelings** as well as of brain events, **and of persons** (and so their essential immaterial parts, souls) as well as of bodies.

These arguments which show that **humans have two parts—body and soul**—will show that **any creature which has a mental life will also have two parts**. The same issues will arise for a chimpanzee or a cat as for a human. If some cat is to undergo a serious brain operation, the question arises whether the cat has reason to fear the bad experiences and look forward to the good experiences which the post-operation cat will have. That question cannot necessarily be answered merely by knowing what has happened to every molecule in the cat's brain. So we must postulate a cat-soul which is the essential part of the cat, and whose continuation makes for the continuation of the cat. Only when we come to animals without thought or feeling does such a question not arise, and then there is no need to postulate an immaterial part of the animal. Certainly human souls have different capacities from the souls of higher animals (the former can have kinds of thought—thoughts about morality or logic—which the latter cannot have; and form kinds of purpose—e.g. to solve an equation—which the latter cannot). But what my arguments show is that animals who have thought and feeling have as their essential part an immaterial soul.

Just as I do not wish to deny that brain events cause mental events (i.e. events in the soul, once it exists) and vice versa, so I do not necessarily wish to deny that **events in the brain play a role in causing the existence of souls.** At some stage of animal evolution, an animal brain became so complex that that caused the existence of a soul connected to it, and the continued development and operation of that brain sustained the existence of the soul; and, as evolution moves on, similar complexity causes similar souls. The connection between one soul and one brain which gets established is a causal one. It is events in this particular brain which cause events in this particular soul, and events in this particular soul which cause events in this particular brain; this is what the connection between this brain and this soul amounts to.

At which stage of the evolutionary process did animals first start to have souls and so a mental life? We do not know. But fairly clearly their behaviour shows that the mammals do have a mental life. My view is that all the vertebrates have a mental life, because they all have a brain similar to the human brain, which, we know, causes a mental life in us, and their behaviour, too, is best explained in terms of their having feelings and beliefs. Dogs and birds and fish all feel pain. But there is no reason at all to attribute a mental life to viruses and bacteria, nor in my view to ants and beetles. They do not have the kind of brain which we do, nor do we need to attribute feelings and beliefs to them in order to explain their behaviour. It follows that at some one particular moment in evolutionary history there appeared something utterly new—consciousness, a mental life, to be analysed in terms of souls having mental properties.

The reluctance of so many philosophers and scientists to admit that at a particular moment of evolutionary history there came into existence, connected to animal bodies, souls with mental properties seems to me to be due in part to the fact that, if such a thing happened, they are utterly lost for an explanation of how it came to happen. But it is highly irrational to say that something is not there, just because you cannot explain how it came to be there. We should accept the evident fact; and if we cannot explain it, we must just be humble and acknowledge that we are not omniscient. But I am going on to suggest that, although there cannot be an inanimate explanation, of the kind characteristic of the natural sciences, of the occurrence of souls and their mental life, the theist does have an explanation.

No Scientific Explanation

Since brain events cause mental events, and mental events cause brain events, **scientists could perhaps establish a long list of such causal connections in humans**, at any rate. The list would state that brain events of a certain kind cause blue images, and brain events of a different kind cause red images; brain events of one kind cause a belief that $36 \times 2 = 72$, and brain events of another kind cause a strong desire to drink tea; and that a purpose to eat cake together with a belief that cake is in the cupboard cause the brain events which cause leg movements in the direction of the cupboard. And so on. Also, just possibly, scientists could list which primitive brains give rise to consciousness—that is, to souls. The reason why I wrote 'just possibly' is that our only grounds for believing that any other organism—whether some animal whose body was formed by normal sexual processes on earth, or some creature on another planet, or some machine made in a factory—is conscious is provided by the similarity of its behaviour and brain organization to ourselves. We do not have an independent check on whether it is conscious. And when the similarities are not strong—as between frogs, say, and human beings—it is in no way obvious whether the animal is conscious. But let us waive difficulties about how we could establish such things, and suppose that we have lists of causal connections between brain events and mental events, and lists of which kinds of primitive brain give rise to consciousness—that is, souls—in which subsequent brain events cause subsequent mental events, and mental events cause brain events.

So there are the phenomena. The problem is to explain them. Why does the formation of a brain of a complexity as great as or greater than that of a certain animal (perhaps an early vertebrate) give rise to consciousness—that is, to a soul with mental states? And why do brain events give rise to the particular mental events they do? Why does a brain event of this kind cause a blue image, and one of that kind cause a red image, and not vice versa? Why does eating chocolate cause the brain events which cause the taste we call chocolatey rather than the taste we call pineapply? A mere list of correlations would be like a list of sentences of a foreign language which translate sentences of English, without any grammar or word dictionary to explain why those sentences are correct translations. And, in the absence of a grammar and dictionary, you are in no position to translate any new sentence.

To provide an inanimate explanation of these phenomena we would need a scientific soul–body theory which satisfied the criteria described in Chapter 2. It would contain a few simple laws from which it would follow that this nerve or computer or other material network would give rise to a soul, and that one would not; that this brain event would cause a red image and that one a blue image; and that this brain event would cause the thought that Russia is a big country, and that one would cause the thought that every human has his own vocation. And so on. The theory would then enable us to predict which brain events of a new kind would give rise to which mental events of a new kind, and which new kinds of machine would have feelings and which not.

Now what makes a theory of mechanics able to explain a diverse set of mechanical phenomena is that the laws of mechanics all deal with the same sort of thing—material objects, their mass, shape, size, and position, and change of mass, shape, size, and position. And material objects differ from each other in respect of these properties in measurable ways (one has twice as much mass as another, or is three times as long as another). Because the properties are measurable, we can have general laws which relate two or more measured quantities in all bodies by a mathematical formula. We do not merely have to say that, when an object of this mass and this velocity collides with an object of that mass and that velocity, such and such results; and so on for innumerable different objects. We can have a general formula, a law saying that for every pair of material objects in collision the quantity of the sum of the mass of the first multiplied by its velocity plus the mass of the second multiplied by its velocity is always conserved. But that can hold only if mass can be measured on a scale—for example, of grams or pounds; and likewise with velocity.

Now a **soul–body theory would deal with very different kinds of thing**. The mass and velocity, and electrical and other physical properties, of material objects are utterly different from the mental (private) properties of thought and feeling which pertain to souls. Physical properties are measurable. So brain events differ from each other in the chemical elements involved in them (which in turn differ from each other in measurable ways) and the speed and direction of the transmission of electric charge. But thoughts do not differ from each other along measurable scales. One thought does not have twice as much of some sort of meaning as another one. So **there could not be a general formula showing the effects of variations in the properties of brain events on mental events**, for the former differ in measurable respects and the latter do not. And what goes for thoughts, goes for mental events of other kinds. A desire for roast beef is not distinguished from a desire for chocolate by having twice as much of something. (Of course, the underlying causes of the one may have twice as much of something as the underlying causes of the other—but that is not the same.) So there could not be a general formula showing how certain variations in brain events produced changes of desires; only a list of which variations in the brain caused which changes of desire and since sensations, thoughts, and so on do not differ from other sensations and thoughts in measurable ways, even more obviously sensations do not differ from thoughts or purposes from beliefs in measurable ways. So there cannot be an explanation deriving from some general formula of why this brain event was caused by a purpose and that one caused a belief, and another one caused a taste of chocolate. Not merely are the kinds of property possessed from time to time by material objects and by souls so different, but, even more obviously, material objects are totally different kinds of things from souls. Souls do not differ from each other or anything else in being made of more or less of some quantity of stuff. So, again, there could be no general formula correlating increase of brain complexity with the occurrence of a soul. Neural networks may become more and more complicated, but there could not be a formula of which it was a consequence that one degree of complexity would not and one just a little greater would give rise to a soul. Having a soul is all-or-nothing (a creature either has some feeling and awareness and so a soul, or no feeling or awareness and so no soul); it cannot be measured. For these reasons there could not be an explanation of soul–brain correlation, a soul–brain science; merely a long list of inexplicable causal connections.

But does not science always surprise us with new discoveries? **The history of science is punctuated with many 'reductions', of one whole branch of science to another** apparently totally different, or 'integration' of apparently very disparate sciences into a super-science. Thermodynamics dealing with heat was reduced to statistical mechanics dealing with velocities of large groups of particles of matter and collisions between them; the temperature of a gas proved to be the mean kinetic energy of its molecules. Optics was reduced to electromagnetism; light proved to be an electromagnetic wave. And the separate sciences of electricity and magnetism came together to form a super-science of electromagnetism. How is it that such great integrations can be achieved if my argument is correct that there cannot be a super-science which explains both mental events and brain-events?

There is a crucial difference between these cases. Every earlier integration into a super-science, of sciences dealing with entities and properties apparently qualitatively very distinct, was achieved by saying that really some of these entities and properties were not as they appeared to be. A distinction was made between the underlying (not immediately observable) material entities and physical properties on the one hand, and the sensory properties to which they gave rise. Thermodynamics was initially concerned with the laws of temperature exchange; and temperature was supposed to be a property inherent in an object which you felt when you touched the object. The felt hotness of a hot body is indeed qualitatively distinct from particle velocities and collisions. The reduction to statistical mechanics was achieved by distinguishing between the underlying cause of the hotness (the motion of molecules) and the sensations which the motion of molecules cause in observers, and saying that really the former was what temperature was, the latter was just the effect of temperature on observers such as us. That done, temperature falls naturally within the scope of statistical mechanics—for molecules are particles; the entities and properties are not now of distinct kinds. Since the two sciences now dealt with entities and properties of the same (measurable) kind, reduction of one to the other now became a practical prospect. But the reduction was achieved at the price of separating off the felt hotness from its causes, and only explaining the latter.

All other 'reductions' of one science to another and 'integrations' of separate sciences dealing with apparently very disparate properties have been achieved by this device of denying that the apparent properties (such as the 'secondary qualities' of colour, heat, sound, taste) with which one science dealt belonged to the physical world at all. It siphoned them off to the world of the mental. But then, when you come to face the problem of the mental events themselves, you cannot do this. If you are to explain the mental events themselves, you cannot distinguish between them and their underlying causes and only explain the latter. In fact, the enormous success of science in producing an integrated physico–chemistry has been achieved at the expense of separating off from the physical world colours, smells, and tastes, and regarding them as purely private sensory phenomena. **What the evidence of the history of science shows is that the way to achieve integration of sciences is to ignore the mental.** The physical world is governed by simple laws (i.e. material objects have the same simple powers and liabilities); the way to discover those laws is to ignore the mental. The very success of science in achieving its vast integrations in physics and chemistry is the very thing which has apparently ruled out any final success in integrating the world of the mind and the world of physics.

As we saw in Chapter 4, the Darwinian theory of evolution by natural selection is able to provide a full explanation of the evolution of human and animal bodies, though not, I argued, a complete or ultimate explanation. But that **Darwinian explanation would explain equally well the evolution of inanimate robots.** Could not Darwinism also tell us something about how the bodies came to be connected with consciousness—that is, souls? Natural selection is a theory of elimination; it explains why so many of the variants thrown up by evolution were eliminated—they were not fitted for survival. But it does not explain why they were thrown up in the first place. In the case of physical variants (such as the length of the giraffe's neck), there is no doubt an adequate explanation in terms of a mutation (a random chemical change) producing a new gene with properties which cause the new variant to appear in accordance with the basic laws of chemistry. But our problem is to explain why some physical state caused the emergence of souls with such mental properties as beliefs, desires, purposes, thoughts, and sensations. Darwinism is of no use in solving this problem.

Darwinian theory might, however, be of use in solving one different problem, and certainly is of use in solving a third problem; but neither of these problems must be confused with the original problem. The first of these additional problems is why, having first appeared in evolutionary history, conscious animals survived. Darwinian theory might be able to show that conscious organisms have some advantage in the struggle for survival over non-conscious organisms programmed to react to their environment in similar ways. It is difficult to see what that could be, but maybe there is an advantage.

The second additional problem is one to which Darwinism can produce a clear, and to my mind fairly obviously correct, answer. That is this problem. Given the existence of mind–brain connections, and given that organisms with a mental life will be favoured in the struggle for survival, why are the brain events which cause and are caused by mental events connected with other bodily events and extra-bodily events in the way in which they are. Take beliefs. A brain event causes the belief that there is a table present. That brain event is caused by a nerve impulse along the optic nerve from the eye when a table image is formed in the eye by light rays arriving from a table. But an animal could have evolved in which the brain event which caused the table belief was caused by quite different events in the outside world. Why these particular connections between the brain and the outside world? The answer is evident: animals with beliefs are more likely to survive if their beliefs are largely true. False beliefs—for example, about the location of food or predators—will lead to rapid elimination in the struggle for food or predators. If you believe that there is no table present, when there is one, you will fall over it, and so on. Those in whom the brain states which give rise to beliefs are connected by causal chains to the outside world, in such a way that the causal chain is normally only activated by a state of affairs which causes the brain state, which in turn causes the belief that the state of affairs holds, will normally hold true beliefs about the world and in consequence be more likely to survive. Similarly, given that I am going to have desires caused by brain events, there are evolutionary advantages in my having some under some circumstances rather than others under other circumstances—for example, desire for food when I am hungry rather than when I am satiated. The same kind of account can be given of why the brain events produced by purposes give rise to the movements of a body purposed. If, when I tried to move my foot, my hand moved instead, predators would soon overtake me. But this correct explanation of why (given that brain events cause mental events) the brain is connected by nerves to the rest of the body in the way it is does not explain why brain events cause mental events, which is a quite different problem. And similarily for why mental events cause brain events.

So then, in summary, the evolution of the mental life of animals (i.e. animals having souls with certain mental events) involves:

(a) there existing certain physical–mental connections (certain physical events causing the existence of souls with certain mental properties, and conversely);

(b) there existing animals with brains whose states give rise to souls having an advantage in the struggle for survival;

(c) evolution selecting animals whose brains are 'wired in' to their bodies in certain ways.

Darwinian mechanisms can explain (c), and possibly (b): but neither Darwinism nor any other science has much prospect of explaining (a). The origination of the most novel and striking features of animals (their conscious life of feeling, choice, and reason) seem to lie utterly beyond the range of science.

Yet there are these causal connections between soul and brain which do not seem to arise from the powers and liabilities of material objects of a kind that science can explain. There are causal connections between particular kinds of brain event and particular kinds of mental event; and causal connections between brain events and the very existence of souls.

I must however now qualify even the latter claim. It may well be that certain primitive brain states cause the existence of souls—as **the foetal brain** reaches a certain state of development it gives rise to a soul connected with it. But what it **could not cause** is—**which soul is connected with it.** It could not be the powers of this brain, of the molecules of this foetus arising from these genes, which cause it to be the case that *my* soul is connected to this brain and yours to that, rather than vice versa. It would be equally compatible with all the regularities between kinds of event (this kind of brain organization and the existence of a kind of thing—a soul) that science could ever discover that you and I should have been connected to brains in the opposite way to the way in which we are connected. There simply is no possible scientific discovery which anyone could ever imagine which would explain why it happened this way rather than that way. Once the connection is made, we begin to become suited to the particular brain; connected to a male brain, I begin to have male thoughts. But that has no relevance to the question of why the 'I' of unformed character was fitted to a male rather than to a female brain. Here science simply stops.

Theistic Explanation

But **theism can provide an explanation of these things**. God, being omnipotent, is able to join souls to bodies. He can cause there to be the particular brain event–mental event connections which there are. He can do this by causing molecules when formed into brains to have powers to produce mental events in souls to which they are connected, and the liabilities to execute the purposes of such connected souls (new powers and liabilities not deriving from the ordinary ones which chemistry analyses). And he can make the souls in the first place and choose to which brain (and so body) each soul is to be connected when foetal brain events require a soul to be connected to the brain.

He has **good reason to cause the existence of souls and join them to bodies**, in the goodness of the existence of embodied animals and human beings who can have enjoyable sensations, satisfy their desires, have their beliefs about what the world is like, and form their own purposes in the light of these beliefs which make a difference to the world. This involves the existence of regular causal connections between mental events and brain events. We cannot make a difference to the world if, each time we try to move our leg, some different effect is caused in the brain and thereby in the body—one time the arm moves, one time we find ourselves sneezing, and so on. Likewise, if we are to discriminate between one object and another, they have to look (feel, etc.) different, and so there has to be a regular causal connection between the brain events caused by objects of each kind and the mental visual impressions of them. And, if we are to have the awesome power of reproduction, there have to be regular connections between our sexual acts, the foetus to which they give rise, and some soul or other linked to that foetus. God has reason to set up all these connections. He may also have a reason to join this soul to this particular body, but, if there is no reason for joining one soul to one body rather than to a different body, he has reason by a 'mental toss up' to produce one-or-other connection—that is, to make it a chance matter which connection holds.

A perfectly good God will love creatures, and love creatures of varying natures—including creatures with narrow ranges of purposes and beliefs, such as rats and dogs. But he has a special reason for producing human beings. **Human beings differ from the higher animals in the kinds of beliefs and purposes they have.** For instance, we have moral beliefs, beliefs about the origin of our existence or fundamental theories of mathematics. We can reason from this to that, and our beliefs are consciously based on other beliefs (we come to have a particular belief about the Romans because we believe that a particular thing was found in Chichester). And our purposes are not just immediate purposes to get food or drink, but purposes to create complicated machines, build beautiful buildings, and purposes to change ourselves and each other—to form our characters so that we are naturally inclined to do this sort of action and not that.

Humans also, I believe, and I suggested in Chapter 1, **have free will**—that is, our purposes are not fully determined by our brain states or anything else. It does seem to us that way, as we choose, that it is up to us how we choose. I should at this stage say something briefly about an objection to this which will occur to the reader. Is not the brain an ordinary material object in which normal scientific laws operate? How, then, can a human freely choose to move his arm or not, or perform any piece of public behaviour, without violating scientific laws? For the way a human moves his arm or does anything public is by bringing about a brain event (unintentionally) and thereby intentionally bringing about the public movement. So, if humans have free will, would they not then be able to prevent normal scientific laws operating in the brain? **One answer** to this is that quite obviously **the brain is not an ordinary material object**, since—unlike ordinary material objects—it gives rise to souls and their mental lives. Hence we would not necessarily expect it to be governed totally by the normal laws of physics which concern ordinary material objects. But a **second answer** is that, even if the brain is governed by the same laws as govern other material objects, that could still be compatible with humans having free will. This is because one of the two great theories of modern physics, **Quantum Theory**, shows that the physical world on the small scale is not fully deterministic. An element of unpredictability governs the behaviour of atoms, and the even smaller electrons, protons and photons, and other fundamental particles out of which atoms are made. This unpredictability is not just a limit to human ability to predict effects, but, if Quantum Theory is true, a limit to the extent to which material objects have precise effects, a limit to the extent to which the physical world is deterministic. Exactly how an electron or photon will move is unpredictable, though we can often say that it is more probable that it will move along one path than along another path. Likewise atoms of one kind often 'decay', turning into atoms of another kind. All that Quantum Theory can tell us is how probable it is that an atom of, say, radium will decay within a given time, not exactly when it will decay. But, while such unpredictability at the atomic level does not normally give rise to any significant unpredictability on the larger scale, it can do so. We could construct a machine which would ensure that, if some atom decayed within a certain time, a nuclear bomb would explode but otherwise it would not. Then we could not predict whether the bomb would explode or not. Now the brain is an intricate machine which also magnifies small changes, and it may well be like this: that the unpredictable small changes in the brain are the ones which cause our thought and observable behaviour. In that case, when humans form their purposes to think of this or that or behave in such and such a way, they thereby cause those small changes unpredictable by science which in turn cause the thought and behaviour. In this way, humans can exercise free will without their doing so involving any violation of the physical laws which govern the brain. These two answers suggest that there is no reason from physics for supposing that things are not as they seem to be with respect to free human choice.

So we humans have great possibilities for acquiring true and deep beliefs about the world and for moulding not just our environment on the large scale in complex ways, but also ourselves. In so many different ways we can choose between good and evil, and our choices make a big difference. A generous God has reason to create such beings.

The evidence deployed in this chapter suggests that the existence of souls and their connections to bodies are not due to the physical processes codified in natural laws. Some new powers have been given to foetal brains, and to the souls to which they are joined, powers which do not have a scientific explanation. The existence of God, a simple hypothesis which leads us with some probability to expect the phenomena discussed in the last chapter, also leads us to expect these phenomena. Hence they constitute further evidence for his existence. Although the powers of the brain and its liability to exercise these when it receives certain nerve impulses from the eye provide a full explanation of my having a blue image when I do, those powers are created and conserved by God, and so his action provides the ultimate explanation of the occurrence of the blue image. God's action also provides the ultimate explanation of there being a soul (and it being my soul rather than yours) which is joined to this body. It has been a common (though not universal) Christian doctrine that, while God operates through 'secondary causes' (i.e. natural processes) to do much else in the world, he intervenes directly to create human souls and link them to bodies. I have gone beyond it to suggest that the same is true of the souls of the higher animals.

6

WHY GOD ALLOWS EVIL

This world is a clearly providential world in this sense—that we humans can have a great influence on our own destiny, and on the destiny of our world and its other inhabitants; and it is very good for us that it is like that. And yet animals and humans suffer (through natural processes of disease and accident), and they cause each other to suffer (we hurt and maim each other and cause each other to starve). The world, that is, contains much evil. An omnipotent God could have prevented this evil, and surely a perfectly good and omnipotent God would have done so. So why is there this evil? Is not its existence strong evidence against the existence of God? It would be unless we can construct what is known as a theodicy, an explanation of why God would allow such evil to occur. I believe that that can be done, and **I shall outline a theodicy in this chapter**. I emphasize that in this chapter, as in Chapter 1, in writing that God would do this or that, I am not taking for granted the existence of God, but merely claiming that, if there is a God, it is to be expected that he would do certain things, including allowing the occurrence of certain evils; and so, I am claiming, their occurrence is not evidence against his existence.

It is inevitable that any attempt by myself or anyone else to construct a theodicy will sound callous, indeed totally insensitive to human suffering. Many theists, as well as atheists, have felt that any attempt to construct a theodicy evinces an immoral approach to suffering. I can only ask the reader to believe that I am not totally insensitive to human suffering, and that I do mind about the agony of poisoning, child abuse, bereavement, solitary imprisonment, and marital infidelity as much as anyone else. True, I would not in most cases recommend that a pastor give this chapter to victims of sudden distress at their worst moment, to read for consolation. But this is not because its arguments are unsound; it is simply that most people in deep distress need comfort, not argument. Yet there is a problem about why God allows evil, and, if the theist does not have (in a cool moment) a satisfactory answer to it, then his belief in God is less than rational, and there is no reason why the atheist should share it. To appreciate the argument of this chapter, each of us needs to stand back a bit from the particular situation of his or her own life and that of close relatives and friends (which can so easily seem the only important thing in the world), and ask very generally what good things would a generous and everlasting God give to human beings in the course of a short earthly life. Of course thrills of pleasure and periods of contentment are good things, and—other things being equal—God would certainly seek to provide plenty of those. But a generous God will seek to give deeper good things than these. He will seek to give us great responsibility for ourselves, each other, and the world, and thus a share in his own creative activity of determining what sort of world it is to be. And he will seek to make our lives valuable, of great use to ourselves and each other. The problem is that **God cannot give us these goods in full measure without allowing much evil on the way.**

The problem of evil is not that of the absence of various good states. We noted in Chapter 1 that, however much good God creates, he could create more; and he does not in general have any obligation to create. That is why death is not in itself an evil; death is just the end of a good state, life (and in any case one of which God may choose to give us more—by giving us a life after death). Death may be an evil if it comes prematurely, or causes great grief to others; but in itself it is not an evil. But there are plenty of evils, positive bad states, which God could if he chose remove. I divide these into moral evils and natural evils. I understand by '**natural evil**' all evil which is not deliberately produced by human beings and which is not allowed by human beings to occur as a result of their negligence. Natural evil includes both physical suffering and mental suffering, of animals as well as humans; all the trail of suffering which disease, natural disasters, and accidents unpredictable by humans bring in their train. 'Moral evil' I understand as including all evil caused deliberately by humans doing what they ought not to do (or allowed to occur by humans negligently failing to do what they ought to do) *and* also the evil constituted by such deliberate actions or negligent failure. It includes the sensory pain of the blow inflicted by the bad parent on his child, the mental pain of the parent depriving the child of love, the starvation allowed to occur in Africa because of negligence by members of foreign governments who could have prevented it, and also the evil of the parent or politician deliberately bringing about the pain or not trying to prevent the starvation.

Moral Evil

The central core of any theodicy must, I believe, be the 'free-will defence', which deals—to start with—with moral evil, but can be extended to deal with much natural evil as well. **The free-will defence** claims that it is a great good that humans have a certain sort of free will which I shall call free and responsible choice, but that, if they do, then necessarily there will be the natural possibility of moral evil. (By the 'natural possibility' I mean that it will not be determined in advance whether or not the evil will occur.) A God who gives humans such free will necessarily bring about the possibility, and puts outside his own control whether or not that evil occurs. It is not logically possible—that is, it would be self-contradictory to suppose—that God could give us such free will and yet ensure that we always use it in the right way.

Free and responsible choice is not just free will in the narrow sense of being able to choose between alternative actions, without our choice being causally necessitated by some prior cause. I have urged, for the reasons given in the last chapter, that humans do have such free will. But humans could have that kind of free will merely in virtue of being able to choose freely between two equally good and unimportant alternatives.

Free and responsible choice is rather free will (of the kind discussed) to make significant choices between good and evil, which make a big difference to the agent, to others, and to the world.

Given that we have free will, we certainly have free and responsible choice. Let us remind ourselves of the difference that humans can make to themselves, others, and the world. Humans have opportunities to give themselves and others pleasurable sensations, and to pursue worthwhile activities—to play tennis or the piano, to acquire knowledge of history and science and philosophy, and to help others to do so, and thereby to build deep personal relations founded upon such sensations and activities. And **humans are so made that they can form their characters**. Aristotle famously remarked: 'we become just by doing just acts, prudent by doing prudent acts, brave by doing brave acts'. That is, by doing a just act when it is difficult—when it goes against our natural inclinations (which is what I understand by desires)—we make it easier to do a just act next time. We can gradually change our desires, so that—for example—doing just acts becomes natural. Thereby we can free ourselves from the power of the less good desires to which we are subject. And, by choosing to acquire knowledge and to use it to build machines of various sorts, humans can extend the range of the differences they can make to the world—they can build universities to last for centuries, or save energy for the next generation; and by co-operative effort over many decades they can eliminate poverty. The possibilities for free and responsible choice are enormous.

It is **good that the free choices of humans should include genuine responsibility for other humans, and that involves the opportunity to benefit or harm them**. God has the power to benefit or to harm humans. If other agents are to be given a share in his creative work, it is good that they have that power too (although perhaps to a lesser degree). A world in which agents can benefit each other but not do each other harm is one where they have only very limited responsibility for each other. If my responsibility for you is limited to whether or not to give you a camcorder, but I cannot cause you pain, stunt your growth, or limit your education, then I do not have a great deal of responsibility for you. A God who gave agents only such limited responsibilities for their fellows would not have given much. God would have reserved for himself the all-important choice of the kind of world it was to be, while simply allowing humans the minor choice of filling in the details. He would be like a father asking his elder son to look after the younger son, and adding that he would be watching the elder son's every move and would intervene the moment the elder son did a thing wrong. The elder son might justly retort that, while he would be happy to share his father's work, he could really do so only if he were left to make his own judgements as to what to do within a significant range of the options available to the father. A good God, like a good father, will delegate responsibility. In order to allow creatures a share in creation, he will allow them the choice of hurting and maiming, of frustrating the divine plan. Our world is one where creatures have just such deep responsibility for each other. I can not only benefit my children, but harm them. One way in which I can harm them is that I can inflict physical pain on them. But there are much more damaging things which I can do to them. Above all I can stop them growing into creatures with significant knowledge, power, and freedom; I can determine whether they come to have the kind of free and responsible choice which I have. The possibility of humans bringing about significant evil is a logical consequence of their having this free and responsible choice. Not even God could give us this choice without the possibility of resulting evil.

Now, as we saw in Chapter 1, an action would not be intentional unless it was done for a reason—that is, seen as in some way a good thing (either in itself or because of its consequences). And, if reasons alone influence actions, that regarded by the subject as most important will determine what is done; an agent under the influence of reason alone will inevitably do the action which he regards as overall the best. If an agent does not do the action which he regards as overall the best, he must have allowed factors other than reason to exert an influence on him. In other words, he must have allowed desires for what he regards as good only in a certain respect, but not overall, to influence his conduct. So, **in order to have a choice between good and evil, agents**

need already a certain depravity, in the sense of a system of desires for what they correctly believe to be evil. I need to *want* to overeat, get more than my fair share of money or power, indulge my sexual appetites even by deceiving my spouse or partner, want to see you hurt, if I am to have choice between good and evil. This depravity is itself an evil which is a necessary condition of the greater good. It makes possible a choice made seriously and deliberately, because made in the face of a genuine alternative. I stress that, according to the free-will defence, it is the natural possibility of moral evil which is the necessary condition of the great good, not the actual evil itself. Whether that occurs is (through God's choice) outside God's control and up to us.

Note further and crucially that, if I suffer in consequence of your freely chosen bad action, that is not by any means pure loss for me. In a certain respect it is a good for *me*. My suffering would be pure loss for me if the only good thing in life was sensory pleasure, and the only bad thing sensory pain; and it is because the modern world tends to think in those terms that the problem of evil seems so acute. If these were the only good and bad things, the occurrence of suffering would indeed be a conclusive objection to the existence of God. But we have already noted the great good of freely choosing and influencing our future, that of our fellows, and that of the world. And now note another great good—the good of our life serving a purpose, of being of use to ourselves and others. Recall the words of Christ, 'it is more blessed to give than to receive' (as quoted by St Paul (Acts 20: 35)). We tend to think, when the beggar appears on our doorstep and we feel obliged to give and do give, that that was lucky for him but not for us who happened to be at home. That is not what Christ's words say. They say that *we* are the lucky ones, not just because we have a lot, out of which we can give a little, but because we are privileged to contribute to the beggar's happiness—and that privilege is worth a lot more than money. And, just as it is a great good freely to choose to do good, so it is also a good to be used by someone else for a worthy purpose (so long, that is, that he or she has the right, the authority, to use us in this way). **Being allowed to suffer to make possible a great good is a privilege**, even if the privilege is forced upon you. Those who are allowed to die for their country and thereby save their country from foreign oppression are privileged. Cultures less obsessed than our own by the evil of purely physical pain have always recognized that. And they have recognized that it is still a blessing, even if the one who died had been conscripted to fight.

And even twenty-first-century man can begin to see that— sometimes—when he seeks to help prisoners, not by giving them more comfortable quarters, but by letting them help the handicapped; or when he pities rather than envies the 'poor little rich girl' who has everything and does nothing for anyone else. And one phenomenon prevalent at the beginning of twenty-first-century Britain draws this especially to our attention—the evil of unemployment. Because of our system of Social Security, the unemployed on the whole have enough money to live without too much discomfort; certainly they are a lot better off than are many employed in Africa or Asia or Victorian Britain. What is evil about unemployment is not so much any resulting poverty but the uselessness of the unemployed. They often report feeling unvalued by society, of no use, 'on the scrap heap'. They rightly think it would be a good for them to contribute; but they cannot. Many of them would welcome a system where they were obliged to do useful work in preference to one where society has no use for them.

It follows from that fact that being of use is a benefit for him who is of use, that those who suffer at the hands of others and thereby make possible the good of those others who have free and responsible choice, are themselves benefited in this respect. I am fortunate if the natural possibility of my suffering if you choose to hurt me is the vehicle which makes your choice really matter. My vulnerability, my openness to suffering (which necessarily involves my actually suffering if you make the wrong choice), means that you are not just like a pilot in a simulator, where it does not matter if mistakes are made. That our choices matter tremendously, that we can make great differences to things for good or ill, is one of the greatest gifts a creator can give us. And if my suffering is the means by which he can give you that choice, I too am in this respect fortunate. Though of course suffering is in itself a bad thing, my good fortune is that the suffering is not random, pointless suffering. It is suffering which is a consequence of my vulnerability which makes me of such use.

Someone may object that the only good thing is not *being* of use (dying for one's country or being vulnerable to suffering at your hands), but *believing* that one is of use—believing that one is dying for one's country and that this is of use; the 'feel-good' experience. But that cannot be correct. Having comforting beliefs is only a good thing if they are true beliefs. It is not a good thing to believe that things are going well when they are not, or that your life is of use when it is not. Getting pleasure out of a comforting falsehood is a cheat. But if I get pleasure out of a true belief, it must be that I regard the state of things which I believe to hold to be a good thing. If I get pleasure out of the true belief that my daughter is doing well at school, it must be that I regard it as a good thing that my daughter does well at school (whether or not I believe that she is doing well). If I did not think the latter, I would not get any pleasure out of believing that she is doing well. Likewise, the belief that I am vulnerable to suffering at your hands, and that that is a good thing, can only be a good thing if **being vulnerable to suffering at your hands is itself a good thing (independently of whether I believe it or not)**. Certainly, when my life is of use and that is a good for me, it is even better if I believe it and get comfort therefrom; but it can only be even better if it is already a good for me whether I believe it or not.

But though suffering may in these ways serve good purposes, **does God have the right to allow me to suffer for your benefit**, without asking my permission? For surely, an objector will say, no one has the right to allow one person A to suffer for the benefit of another one B without A's consent. We judge that doctors who use patients as involuntary objects of experimentation in medical experiments, which they hope will produce results that can be used to benefit others are doing something wrong. After all, if my arguments about the utility of suffering are sound, ought we not all to be causing suffering to others in order that those others may have the opportunity to react in the right way?

There are, however, crucial differences between God and the doctors. The first is that **God as the author of our being has certain rights**, a certain authority **over us, which we do not have over our fellow humans**. He is the cause of our existence at each moment of our existence and sustains the laws of nature which give us everything we are and have. To allow someone to suffer for his own good or that of others, one has to stand in some kind of parental relationship towards him. I do not have the right to let some stranger suffer for the sake of some good, when I could easily prevent this, but I do have *some* right of this kind in respect of my own children. I may let the younger son suffer *somewhat* for his own good or that of his brother. I have this right because in small part I am responsible for the younger son's existence, his beginning and continuance. If I have begotten him, nourished, and educated him, I have some limited rights over him in return; to a *very limited* extent I can use him for some worthy purpose. If this is correct, then a God who is so much more the author of our being than are our parents has so much more right in this respect. But doctors do not have over their patients even the limited rights that parents have over their children.

But secondly and all-importantly, the doctors *could* have asked the patients for permission; and the patients, being free agents of some power and knowledge, could have made an informed choice of whether or not to allow themselves to be used. By contrast, **God's choice is** not about how to use already existing agents, but **about the sort of agents to make and the sort of world into which to put them**. In God's situation there are no agents to be asked. I am arguing that it is good that one agent A should have deep responsibility for another B (who in turn could have deep responsibility for another C). It is not logically possible for God to have asked B if he wanted things thus, for, if A is to be responsible for B's growth in freedom, knowledge, and power, there will not be a B with enough freedom and knowledge to make any choice, before God has to choose whether or not to give A responsibility for him. One cannot ask a baby into which sort of world he or she wishes to be born. The creator has to make the choice independently of his creatures. He will seek on balance to benefit them—all of them. And, in giving them the gift of life—whatever suffering goes with it—that is a substantial benefit. But when one suffers at the hands of another, often perhaps it is not enough of a benefit to outweigh the suffering. Here is the point to recall that it is an additional benefit to the sufferer that his suffering is the means whereby the one who hurt him had the opportunity to make a significant choice between good and evil which otherwise he would not have had.

Although for these reasons, as I have been urging, God has the right to allow humans to cause each other to suffer, **there must be a limit to the amount of suffering** which he has the right to allow a human being to suffer for the sake of a great good. A parent may allow an elder child to have the power to do some harm to a younger child for the sake of the responsibility given to the elder child; but there are limits. And there are limits even to the moral right of God, our creator and sustainer, to use free sentient beings as pawns in a greater game. Yet, if these limits were too narrow, God would be unable to give humans much real responsibility; he would be able to allow them only to play a toy game. Still, limits there must be to God's rights to allow humans to hurt each other; and limits there are in the world to the extent to which they can hurt each other, provided above all by the short finite life enjoyed by humans and other creatures—one human can hurt another for no more than eighty years or so. And there are a number of other safety-devices in-built into our physiology and psychology, limiting the amount of pain we can suffer. But the primary safety limit is that provided by the shortness of our finite life. Unending unchosen suffering would indeed to my mind provide a very strong argument against the existence of God. But that is not the human situation.

So then God, without asking humans, has to choose for them between the kinds of world in which they can live—basically either a world in which there is very little opportunity for humans to benefit or harm each other, or a world in which there is considerable opportunity. How shall he choose? There are clearly reasons for both choices. But it seems to me (just, on balance) that his choosing to create the world in which we have considerable opportunity to benefit or harm each other is to bring about a good at least as great as the evil which he thereby allows to occur. *Of course* the suffering he allows is a bad thing; and, other things being equal, to be avoided. But having the natural possibility of causing suffering makes possible a greater good. God, in creating humans who (of logical necessity) cannot choose for themselves the kind of world into which they are to come, plausibly exhibits his goodness in making for them the heroic choice that they come into a risky world where they may have to suffer for the good of others.

Natural Evil

Natural evil is not to be accounted for along the same lines as moral evil. Its main role rather, I suggest, is to make it possible for humans to have the kind of choice which the free-will defence extols, and to make available to humans specially worthwhile kinds of choice.

There are two ways in which natural evil operates to give humans those choices. First, **the operation of natural laws producing evils gives humans knowledge** (if they choose to seek it) of how to bring about such evils themselves. Observing you catch some disease by the operation of natural processes gives me the power either to use those processes to give that disease to other people, or through negligence to allow others to catch it, or to take measures to prevent others from catching the disease. Study of the mechanisms of nature producing various evils (and goods) opens up for humans a wide range of choice. This is the way in which in fact we learn how to bring about (good and) evil. But could not God give us the requisite knowledge (of how to bring about good or evil) which we need in order to have free and responsible choice by a less costly means? Could he not just whisper in our ears from time to time what are the different consequences of different actions of ours? Yes. But anyone who believed that an action of his would have some effect because he believed that God had told him so would see all his actions as done under the all-watchful eye of God. He would not merely believe strongly that there was a God, but would know it with real certainty. That knowledge would greatly inhibit his freedom of choice, would make it very difficult for him to choose to do evil. This is because we all have a natural inclination to wish to be thought well of by everyone, and above all by an all-good God; that we have such an inclination is a very good feature of humans, without which we would be less than human. Also, if we were directly informed of the consequences of our actions, we would be deprived of the choice whether to seek to discover what the consequences were through experiment and hard cooperative work. Knowledge would be available on tap. Natural processes alone give humans knowledge of the effects of their actions without inhibiting their freedom, and if evil is to be a possibility for them they must know how to allow it to occur.

The other way in which **natural** evil operates to give humans their freedom is that it **makes possible certain kinds of action towards it between which agents can choose**. It increases the range of significant choice. A particular natural evil, such as physical pain, gives to the sufferer a choice—whether to endure it with patience, or to bemoan his lot. His friend can choose whether to show compassion towards the sufferer, or to be callous. The pain makes possible these choices, which would not otherwise exist. There is no guarantee that our actions in response to the pain will be good ones, but the pain gives us the opportunity to perform good actions. The good or bad actions which we perform in the face of natural evil themselves provide opportunities for further choice—of good or evil stances towards the former actions. If I am patient with my suffering, you can choose whether to encourage or laugh at my patience; if I bemoan my lot, you can teach me by word and example what a good thing patience is. If you are sympathetic, I have then the opportunity to show gratitude for the sympathy; or to be so self-involved that I ignore it. If you are callous, I can choose whether to ignore this or to resent it for life. And so on. I do not think that there can be much doubt that natural evil, such as physical pain, makes available these sorts of choice. The actions which natural evil makes possible are ones which allow us to perform at our best and interact with our fellows at the deepest level.

It may, however, be suggested that adequate opportunity for these great good actions would be provided by the occurrence of moral evil without any need for suffering to be caused by natural processes. You can show courage when threatened by a gunman, as well as when threatened by cancer; and show sympathy to those likely to be killed by gunmen as well as to those likely to die of cancer. But just imagine all the suffering of mind and body caused by disease, earthquake, and accident unpreventable by humans removed at a stroke from our society. No sickness, no bereavement in consequence of the untimely death of the young. Many of us would then have such an easy life that we simply would not have much opportunity to show courage or, indeed, manifest much in the way of great goodness at all. We need those insidious processes of decay and dissolution which money and strength cannot ward off for long to give us the opportunities, so easy otherwise to avoid, to become heroes.

God has the right to allow natural evils to occur (for the same reason as he has the right to allow moral evils to occur)—up to a limit. It would, of course, be crazy for God to multiply evils more and more in order to give endless opportunity for heroism, but to have *some* significant opportunity for real heroism and consequent character formation is a benefit for the person to whom it is given. Natural evils give to us the knowledge to make a range of choices between good and evil, and the opportunity to perform actions of especially valuable kinds.

There is, however, no reason to suppose that **animals** have free will. So **what about their suffering?** Animals had been suffering for a long time before humans appeared on this planet—just how long depends on which animals are conscious beings. The first thing to take into account here is that, while the higher animals, at any rate the vertebrates, suffer, it is most unlikely that they suffer nearly as much as humans do. Given that suffering depends directly on brain events (in turn caused by events in other parts of the body), then, since the lower animals do not suffer at all and humans suffer a lot, animals of intermediate complexity (it is reasonable to suppose) suffer only a moderate amount. So, while one does need a theodicy to account for why God allows animals to suffer, one does not need as powerful a theodicy as one does in respect of humans. One only needs reasons adequate to account for God allowing an amount of suffering much less than that of humans. That said, there is, I believe, available for animals parts of the theodicy which I have outlined above for humans.

The good of animals, like that of humans, does not consist solely in thrills of pleasure. For animals, too, there are more worthwhile things, and in particular intentional actions, and among them serious significant intentional actions. The life of animals involves many serious significant intentional actions. Animals look for a mate, despite being tired and failing to find one. They take great trouble to build nests and feed their young, to decoy predators and explore. But all this inevitably involves pain (going on despite being tired) and danger. An animal cannot intentionally avoid forest fires, or take trouble to rescue its offspring from forest fires, unless there exists a serious danger of getting caught in a forest fire. The action of rescuing despite danger simply cannot be done unless the danger exists—and the danger will not exist unless there is a significant natural probability of being caught in the fire. Animals do not choose freely to do such actions, but the actions are nevertheless worthwhile. It is great that animals feed their young, not just themselves; that animals explore when they know it to be dangerous; that animals save each other from predators, and so on. These are the things that give the lives of animals their value. But they do often involve some suffering to some creatures.

To return to the central case of humans—the reader will agree with me to the extent to which he or she values responsibility, free choice, and being of use very much more than thrills of pleasure or absence of pain. There is no other way to get the evils of this world into the right perspective, except to reflect at length on innumerable, very detailed thought experiments (in addition to actual experiences of life) in which we postulate very different sorts of worlds from our own, and then ask ourselves whether the perfect goodness of God would require him to create one of these (or no world at all) rather than our own. But **I conclude with a very small thought experiment**, which may help to begin this process. Suppose that you exist in another world before your birth in this one, and are given a choice as to the sort of life you are to have in this one. You are told that you are to have only a short life, maybe of only a few minutes, although it will be an adult life in the sense that you will have the richness of sensation and belief characteristic of adults. You have a choice as to the sort of life you will have. You can have either a few minutes of very considerable pleasure, of the kind produced by some drug such as heroin, which you will experience by yourself and which will have no effects at all in the world (for example, no one else will know about it); or you can have a few minutes of considerable pain, such as the pain of childbirth, which will have (unknown to you at the time of pain) considerable good effects on others over a few years. You are told that, if you do not make the second choice, those others will never exist—and so you are under no moral obligation to make the second choice. But you seek to make the choice which will make *your* own life the best life for *you* to have led. How will you choose? The choice is, I hope, obvious. You should choose the second alternative.

For someone who remains unconvinced by my claims about the relative strengths of the good and evils involved—holding that, great though the goods are, they do not justify the evils which they involve—there is a fall-back position. My arguments may have convinced you of the greatness of the goods involved sufficiently for you to allow that a perfectly good God would be justified in bringing about the evils for the sake of the good which they make possible, if and only if God also provided **compensation in the form of happiness after death to the victims whose sufferings make possible the goods**. Someone whose theodicy requires buttressing in this way will need an independent reason for believing that God does provide such life after death if he is to be justified in holding his theodicy, and I shall mention briefly in the next chapter the sort of reason that might be. While believing that God does provide at any rate for many humans such life after death, I have expounded a theodicy without relying on this assumption. But I can understand someone thinking that the assumption is needed, especially when we are considering the worst evils. (This compensatory afterlife need not necessarily be the everlasting life of Heaven.)

It remains the case, however, that evil is evil, and there is a substantial price to pay for the goods of our world which it makes possible. God would not be less than perfectly good if he created instead a world without pain and suffering, and so without the particular goods which those evils make possible. Christian, Islamic, and much Jewish tradition claims that God has created worlds of both kinds—our world, and the **Heaven** of the blessed. The latter is a marvellous world with a vast range of possible deep goods, but it lacks a few goods which our world contains, including the good of being able to reject the good. A generous God might well choose to give some of us the choice of rejecting the good in a world like ours before giving to those who embrace it a wonderful world in which the former possibility no longer exists.

7

HOW THE EXISTENCE OF GOD EXPLAINS MIRACLES AND RELIGIOUS EXPERIENCE

Miracles

I have argued so far that the claim that God created and sustains our universe is the hypothesis that best accounts for its general structure—its very existence, its conformity to natural laws, its being fine-tuned to evolve animals and humans, and these latter being conscious beings with sensations, thoughts, beliefs, desires, and purposes who can make great differences to themselves and the world in deeply significant ways. I have argued too that the existence of evil of the kind we find on earth does not count against that claim. The evidence considered so far, therefore, gives a significant degree of probability to that claim—that there is a God. However, if there is a God, who, being perfectly good, will love his creatures, **one would expect God to interact with us occasionally more directly on a personal basis**, rather than merely through the natural order of the world which he constantly sustains—to answer our prayers and to meet our needs. **He will not**, however, **intervene in the natural order at all often**, for, if he did, we would not be able to predict the consequences of our actions and so we would lose control over the world and ourselves. If God answered most prayers for a relative to recover from cancer, then cancer would no longer be a problem for humans to solve. Humans would no longer see cancer as a problem to be solved by scientific research—prayer would be the obvious method of curing cancer. God would then have deprived us of the serious choice of whether to put money and energy into finding a cure for cancer or not to bother; and of whether to take trouble to avoid cancer (e.g. by not smoking) or not to bother. Natural laws determining that certain events will cause good effects and other ones cause bad effects enable us to discover which produce which and to use them for ourselves. Natural laws are like rules, instituted by parents, schools, or governments, stating that these actions will be punished and those ones rewarded. Once we discover the rules, we acquire control over the consequences of our actions—we can then choose whether to be rewarded or to risk being punished. But loving parents will rightly occasionally break their own rules in answer to special pleading—it means that they are persons in interaction, not just systems of rules. And for a similar reason one might expect God occasionally to break his own rules, and intervene in history.

One might expect God occasionally to answer prayer when it is for a good cause—such as the relief of suffering and restoration to health of mind or body, and for awareness of himself and of important spiritual truths. And one might also expect him to intervene occasionally without waiting for our prayer—to help us to make the world better in various ways when we have misused our freedom. A divine intervention will consist either in God acting in areas where natural laws do not determine what happens (perhaps our mental life is not fully determined by natural laws), or in God temporarily suspending natural laws. Let us call interventions of the latter kind miracles and interventions of the former kind non-miraculous interventions. **A miracle is a violation or suspension of natural laws, brought about by God**. Does human history contain events of a kind which God, if he exists, would be expected to bring about and yet which do not occur as a result of the operation of natural laws? It certainly contains large numbers of events of the kind which God would be expected to bring about, but about which we have no idea whether they occurred as a result of the operation of natural laws or not. I pray for my friend to get better from cancer and he does. Since we do not normally know in any detail the exact state of his body when he had cancer, nor do we know in any detail the natural laws which govern the development of cancer, we cannot say whether the recovery occurs as a result of natural laws or not. The pious believer believes that God intervened, and the hard-headed atheist believes that only natural laws were at work. Human history also contains *reports* of many events which, *if* they occurred as reported, clearly would not have occurred as a result of natural laws, and which are also events of a kind that God might be expected to bring about. The Second Book of Kings records that a sick and doubting King Hezekiah sought a sign of encouragement from God that he, Hezekiah, would recover and that God would save Jerusalem from the Assyrians. In response to the prayer of the prophet Isaiah that God would give Hezekiah a sign, the shadow cast by the sun reportedly went 'backwards ten steps' (2 Kgs. 20: 11). The latter can only have happened if the laws of mechanics (governing the rotation of the earth on its axis, and so the direction of the sun from Jerusalem), or the laws of light (governing how light from the sun forms shadows in the region of Hezekiah's palace), had been suspended. (In giving this example of an event which, if it occurred as described would have been a miracle, I am not assuming that the event occurred or that it did not occur.)

I suggest that, in so far as we have other reason to believe that there is a God, we have reason to believe that God intervenes in history in some such cases (we may not know which) and so that some of the events happened as described, although not necessitated to do so by natural laws. It would be odd to suppose that God, concerned for our total well-being, confined his interventions to those areas (if any) where natural laws leave it undetermined what will happen—for example, confined his interventions to influencing the mental lives of human beings. If he has reason to interact with us, he has reason very occasionally to intervene to suspend those natural laws by which our life is controlled; and in particular, since the bodily processes which determine our health are fairly evidently subject to largely deterministic natural laws, he has reason very occasionally to intervene in those. Conversely, in so far as we have other reason to believe that there is no God, we have reason to believe that natural processes are the highest-level determinants of what happens and so that no events happen contrary to laws of nature. In other words, background knowledge (our other reasons for general belief about how the world works—e.g. reasons for believing that there is a God, or that there is no God) is rightly a very important factor in assessing what happened on particular occasions (though it is not an important factor in assessing the worth of large scientific or religious theories—see Chapter 2).

But, while background knowledge must be a powerful factor in determining what is reasonable to believe about what happened on particular occasions, it is not, of course, the only factor. We have the detailed historical evidence of what observers seem to recall having happened, what witnesses claim to have observed, and any physical traces of past events (documents, archaeological remains, and so on).

That **background knowledge** must weigh heavily in comparison with the detailed historical evidence in assessing particular claims about the past can be seen from innumerable non-religious examples. If a well-established scientific theory leads you to expect that stars will sometimes explode, then some debris in the sky of a kind which could have been caused by an exploding star but which (though improbably) just might have some other cause may be reasonably interpreted as debris left by an exploding star. But, if a well-established theory says that stars cannot explode, you will need very strong evidence that the debris could not have had another cause before interpreting it as debris of an exploding star. However, in the case of purported miraculous interventions, the background knowledge will be of two kinds. It will include the scientific knowledge of what are the relevant laws of nature—for example, the laws of light and the laws governing the rotation of the earth, which (since laws of nature operate almost all the time) lead us to expect that on that particular occasion Hezekiah's shadow did not move backwards. But it will also include the other evidence that there is a God able and having reason sometimes (but not necessarily on any one particular occasion) to intervene to suspend the operation of natural laws. In view of these conflicting bodies of background knowledge, we would need quite a bit of particular historical evidence to show that, on any particular occasion, God intervened in a miraculous way. The historical evidence could be backed up by argument that that particular purported miracle was one which God had strong reason for bringing about.

To balance **detailed historical evidence** against background knowledge of both kinds to establish what happened on any particular occasion is a difficult matter on which we are seldom going to be able to reach a clear verdict. But detailed historical evidence about what happened could in principle be substantial. To take a simple, imaginary, and not especially religiously significant example, we ourselves might have apparently seen someone levitate (that is, rise in the air, not as a result of strings or magnets or any other known force for which we have checked). Many witnesses, proved totally trustworthy on other occasions where they would have had no reason to lie, might report having observed such a thing. There might even be traces in the form of physical effects which such an event would have caused—for example, marks on the ceiling which would have been caused by a levitating body hitting it. But against all this there will still be the background knowledge of what are the laws of nature, in this case the laws of gravity; and all the evidence in favour of these being the laws of nature will be evidence that they operated at the time in question, and so that no levitation occurred.

Note that any detailed historical evidence that the levitation occurred will, as such, be evidence against the laws of gravity being the laws of nature—just as evidence that some piece of metal did not expand when heated would be evidence that it is not a law of nature that all metals expand when heated. But if, much though we may try, we fail to find further exceptions to our purported law—if, for example, we cannot produce another levitation by recreating the circumstances in which the former one purportedly occurred—that will be grounds for believing that, if the former occurred, it was not an event in accord with some hitherto undiscovered law of nature, but rather a violation or suspension of a law.

In such cases, we would, I think, be most unlikely to have enough detailed historical evidence that the event occurred to outweigh the scientific background knowledge that such events cannot occur, unless we also had substantial religious background knowledge showing not merely that there is a God but that he had very good reason on this particular occasion to work this particular miracle. In the case of a purported levitation, I doubt that we would ever have such evidence. That is not, of course, to say that levitations do not occur, only that we are most unlikely to have enough reason to believe that one did occur on any particular occasion. Note that in all such cases what we are doing is to seek the simplest theory of what happened in the past which leads us to account for the data (what I have here called the detailed historical evidence), and which fits in best with our background knowledge, in the way described in Chapter 2.

I am, however, inclined to think that we do have enough historical evidence of events occurring contrary to natural laws of a kind which God would have reason to bring out to show that probably some of them (we do not know which) are genuine miracles. There are many reports of purported miracles, ancient and modern, some of them quite well documented. (See for example, the cure of the Glasgow man from cancer described in D. Hickey and G. Smith, *Miracle* (1978), or some of the cases discussed in Rex Gardiner, *Healing Miracles* (1986). For a more sceptical account of some purported Lourdes miracles, see, for contrast, D. J. West, *Eleven Lourdes Miracles* (1957). Or, rather, we have enough detailed historical evidence in some such cases given that we have a certain amount of background knowledge to support the claim that there is a God, able and willing to intervene in history. But, of course, the reader must consider the evidence in such cases for himself or herself. The occurrence of such detailed historical evidence is itself further evidence of the existence of God (along with the evidence discussed in Chapters 4 and 5), because one would expect to have it if there is a God but not otherwise—for if natural laws are the highest-level determinants of what happens, there is every reason to expect that they will not be suspended.

It is so often said in such cases that we 'may be mistaken'. New scientific evidence may show that the event as reported was not contrary to natural laws—we simply misunderstood what were the natural laws. Maybe we have just misunderstood how cancer develops; a patient sometimes 'spontaneously' recovers by purely natural processes. Or, if many people claim to have observed someone levitate, maybe they have all been subject to hallucination. Maybe. But the rational enquirer in these matters, as in all matters, must go on the evidence available. If that evidence shows that the laws of nature are such and such, that if the event happened as described it was contrary to them, that the new evidence had no tendency to show that the supposed laws are not the true laws (because in all other similar cases they are followed), that there is very strong historical evidence (witnesses, and so on) that the event occurred, then it is rational to believe that a miracle occurred. We are rational to believe, while allowing the possibility that evidence might turn up later to show that we are mistaken. 'We may be mistaken' is a knife which cuts both ways—**we may be mistaken in believing that an event is not a divine intervention when really it is, as well as the other way round.**

Historians often affirm that, when they are investigating particular claims about past events important to religious traditions—for example, about what Jesus did and what happened to him—they do so without making any religious or anti-religious assumptions. In practice most of them do not live up to such affirmations. Either they heavily discount such biblical claims as that Jesus cured the blind on the grounds that such things do not happen; or (more commonly in past centuries) they automatically accept the testimony of witnesses to what Jesus did, on the grounds that biblical witnesses are especially reliable. But what needs to be appreciated is that background evidence ought to influence the investigator—as it does in all other areas of enquiry. Not to allow it to do so is irrational.

The existence of detailed historical evidence for the occurrence of violations of natural laws of a kind which God, if there is a God, would have had reason to bring about **is itself evidence for the existence of God.** Though not nearly enough on its own, it makes its contribution; and with other evidence (e.g. of the kind considered in Chapters 4 and 5) it could be enough to establish the existence of God. Consider, by analogy, a detective investigating a crime and considering the hypothesis that Jones committed the crime. Some of his clues will be evidence for the occurrence of some event, an event which, if it occurred, would provide evidence in its turn for the hypothesis that Jones committed the crime. The former might, for example, be the evidence of witnesses who claim to have seen Jones near the scene of the crime. Even if Jones was near the scene of the crime, that is in its turn on its own fairly weak evidence that he committed the crime. Much more evidence is needed. But because the testimony of witnesses is evidence for Jones having been near the scene of the crime, and Jones having been near the scene is some evidence that he committed it, the testimony of the witnesses is nevertheless some (indirect) evidence for his having committed the crime. Likewise, evidence of witnesses who claim to observe a violation of natural laws is indirect evidence for the existence of God, because the occurrence of such violations would be itself more direct evidence for the existence of God. If the total evidence becomes strong enough, then it will justify asserting that God exists, and hence that the event in question was not merely a violation, but brought about by God and thus a miracle.

Revelation

One reason which God may have for intervening in history is to inform us of things, to reveal truths to us. Our unaided reason may indeed, as I am arguing in this book, be able to reach the conclusion that probably there is a God; and it may also be able to establish some very general moral truths (e.g. that it is good to feed the starving, whoever they are). But humans are creatures of limited intelligence and notoriously liable to hide from themselves conclusions which seem to stare them in the face when those conclusions are unwelcome. Conclusions about religious and moral matters are ones on which we are so obviously liable to bias because, whatever conclusions we reach (whether religious or atheistic), they have consequences about the sort of life which is worth living; and we may be reluctant to accept them because they clash with our current life-style. **Humans need help**—help to see what our obligations are and what our ultimate good consists in, and help and encouragement to pursue that good. And anyway a God who wants to interact with us will also want to show us things about himself simply in order that we may know him better. The major Western religions all claim that God has intervened in history in order to reveal truths to humans; and they normally add that he has established a mechanism which to some degree or in some way will ensure the preservation of these truths among humans. Jews claim that God intervened in history with Abraham and Moses, and that he revealed truths preserved subsequently by the Jewish people in the Hebrew Scriptures (the Christian Old Testament). Christians accept that, but add that the main divine intervention was that of Jesus Christ, who revealed to us things preserved by the Christian Church in its Bible (the New Testament, and the Old Testament understood in the light of the New). Islam also recognizes to some degree Jewish and even Christian claims, but proclaims Muhammad as the last prophet in whom revelation reached its culmination, a revelation which was recorded in the Qur'an and preserved by Islamic communities.

How are we to judge between these competing claims? In two ways. First, by the plausibility on other grounds of what they claim to be the central revealed doctrines. A religion which advocates large-scale pillage and rape for fun cannot be a true religion. But, while we may be able to pass decisive judgement for or against some claim to revelation on the grounds that it coincides with or clashes with what we can see to be true on other grounds, we cannot do so generally. The claims of purported revelations about what God is like and what he has done will not normally be such that we can have very strong, independent, reason for believing them true or false. The point of revelation is to tell things too deep for our unaided reason to discover. What we need also is some guarantee of a different kind that what is claimed to be revealed really comes from God. To take an analogy, non-scientists cannot test for themselves what physicists tell them about the constitution of the atom. All they can ask for is some guarantee that what they are told comes from someone in a position to know. In the case of a purported revelation from God, that guarantee must take the form of a violation of natural laws which culminates and forwards the proclamation of the purported revelation. Such a violation can only be brought about by him who keeps natural laws going, that is, preserves in objects their powers and liabilities to act—in other words, God. Then the violation will be a miracle. Only he who preserves the powers of things can suspend them; and if their suspension culminates and forwards the proclamation of a purported revelation, that is God's signature on the revelation.

The Christian Revelation

Although the arguments of this book before and subsequent to this section are designed to convince the reader of the existence of the God acknowledged alike by Jews, Muslims, and Christians, and not to make any judgement between their competing claims about him, I am bound to add that in my view only one of the world's major religions can make any serious claim, on the grounds of detailed historical evidence, to be founded on a miracle, and that is the Christian religion. Eastern religions (e.g. Hinduism) sometimes claim divine interventions, but not ones in historical periods for which they can produce many witnesses or writers who have talked to the witnesses. Likewise, although Judaism claims divine interventions connected especially with Moses and the Exodus from Egypt, our information about them was written down long after the events. (And anyway, even if these events occurred as described, it is doubtful whether they would have been miracles. Natural causes may easily account for the East wind which caused the parting of the Red Sea reported in Exodus 14: 21.) And Muslims do not claim that Islam was founded on any miracles, apart from the writing of the Qur'an; and, however great a book that is, it is in no way apparent that writing a great book needs a special divine intervention.

The Christian religion, by contrast, **was founded on the purported miracle of the Resurrection of Jesus**. If this event happened in anything like the way the New Testament books record it as the coming to life of a man dead by crucifixion thirty-six hours earlier, it clearly involved the suspension of natural laws, and so, if there is a God, was brought about by him, and so was a miracle. Most of the books of the New Testament were written during the lifetime of many of those who were involved in the life and death of Jesus. These books were written by various writers who claim that Mary Magdalene, other women, and apostles saw the empty tomb; and that they and many others saw, talked to, and ate with the risen Jesus. The body of Jesus was never produced. Here we have a serious historical claim of a great miracle for which there is a substantial evidence. Just how strong that historical evidence is is a matter on which innumerable books have been written over two millenia, and readers must follow up these issues for themselves in some of these books. But in doing so it is very important to keep in mind three points which I have made on earlier pages.

The first point is that it is a **mark of rationality to take background knowledge**—other evidence about whether there is a God able and willing to intervene in history—**into account**.

The second is that, given that **God does have reason to intervene in** history, **partly in order to reveal truths** about himself, evidence for the truth of the Resurrection must include the plausibility or otherwise of any items clearly taught as central doctrines by Jesus and by the Church founded on the basis of the purported Resurrection. Of course, as I wrote earlier, we will not in general have conclusive independent reasons to believe such central doctrines to be true or false—the point of revelation is to tell us things that we cannot find out for ourselves. But we may have some weak reasons, not adequate by themselves, for believing that, if there is a God, a certain doctrine about what he is like or what he has done or how we ought to behave is true. If we have such reasons, to that extent the doctrines are plausible. I believe that we do have such reasons in the case of central Christian doctrines, such as the teaching of the Sermon of the Mount in its exposition of what goodness consists in, the doctrine of the Trinity, and the doctrines about Jesus—that he was God incarnate (God who had become also a human being), and that his life and death were somehow an atonement for our sins. To discuss these reasons properly would require another book. The sort of reason I have in mind may be illustrated very briefly in the case of the Incarnation. We saw in Chapter 6 that God has reason to allow us to endure much suffering in various ways for the sake of greater goods. If a parent subjects a child to serious suffering for the sake of a greater good to others, then there comes a point at which it is not merely good but obligatory on the parent to show solidarity with the sufferer. Suppose that my country has been unjustly attacked, and the government has introduced conscription in order to raise an army to defend the country. All young men between 18 and 30 are 'called up' to serve in the army; older men under 50 may volunteer. The government however allows parents of those aged between 18 and 21 to 'veto' a call-up. Suppose that I have a 19-year-old son; and, although most parents veto their young sons 'call up', I refuse to do so because of the gravity of the threat to the country's independence. Suppose also that I am 45 years old, and so have no legal obligation to serve. Plausibly since I am forcing my son to endure the hardship and danger of military service, I have a moral obligation to him to volunteer myself. So **it is to be expected that a God who imposes on us much suffering for the sake of great goods will become incarnate**, to share the hardship which he has imposed on us. This is a reason why a divine intervention should take the form, not just of a miracle, but of God himself living a human life. So, if a purported revelation teaches that He did so, that is some mild reason for believing that revelation to be true. Since the Christian Church teaches that God lived and suffered as a human, Jesus (and there is much independent evidence that Jesus suffered much), that is a small reason for believing its doctrines to be God-authenticated and so that Jesus rose from the dead. Conversely, of course, if the reader thinks that he has reason to suppose that, if there is a God, these doctrines would not be true of him, that is reason to suppose that they were not revealed by God, and so that an event claimed to authenticate them did not take place.

Thirdly, the claims of the Christian revelation must be compared with those of other religions. If there is reason (of intrinsic plausibility, or historical evidence for a foundation miracle) to suppose that God has revealed contrary things in the context of another religion, that again is reason to suppose that the Christian revelation is not true, and so that its founding event did not occur. Knowledge is a big web—observations in one field of enquiry can affect what it is reasonable to believe in fields which might at first sight seem very different. My own view—to repeat—is that none of the great religions can make any serious claim on the basis of particular historical evidence for the truth of their purported revelations, apart from the Christian religion. But, of course, if its purported revelation was implausible on other grounds, we would still have to reject it and look elsewhere.

I conclude that, if the reader accepts my judgement that there is serious historical evidence for the founding miracle of Christianity, the Resurrection, and accepts that (however slender) there is some plausibility in its teaching, then—since such a violation of natural laws is to be expected if there is a God—the evidence in favour of that miracle also constitutes further evidence for his existence. This conclusion holds whether or not you think that serious historical evidence would be enough to establish the occurrence of the miracle, without substantial background knowledge. I provide my assessment of the evidence for the Resurrection of Jesus and of the plausibility of Christian teaching more generally in the sequel to this book, *Was Jesus God?*

One item of purported revelation common to Western religions (though not taught by all branches of Judaism) is **the doctrine of life after death**. (This doctrine is taught also by Eastern religions, but many of them do not teach that God will be an important feature of that life.) We humans will live again, and the kind of life we have will depend on how we live in this world. If we seek to be good people and to know

God, then we will be the kind of people naturally fitted for the vision of him in the world to come; and God will provide that vision for us. But if we choose not to pursue goodness and God, then also God will respect our choice and give us a life without God. This doctrine seems to me intrinsically plausible—a perfectly good God might be expected in the end to respect our choice as to the sort of person we choose to be and the sort of life we choose to lead. And, although there is great good in life on Earth, it would be odd if God did not plan something greater and longer for those humans who want it. Hence the fact that this doctrine is taught by each of the great Western religions seems to be evidence in favour of each of them, and so of their common content.

Religious Experience

An omnipotent and perfectly good creator will seek to interact with his creatures and in particular with human persons capable of knowing him. He has reason, as we have seen, to interact in the public world—occasionally making a difference to it in response to our prayers for particular needs. He has reason too to intervene to authenticate a revelation which we badly need. He has reason to make this a public matter, to give a revelation to a community, in order that it may choose to work out its consequences (and iron out apparent minor inconsistencies) through public discussion and propagate it through communal effort. Co-operation in pursuit of the good is an additional good. Yet God also will love each of us as individual creatures, and so has reason to intervene (perhaps in a non-miraculous way, violating no natural laws) simply to show himself to particular individuals, and to tell them things individual to themselves (e.g. to provide for them a vocation). **One would expect there to be religious experiences in the sense of experiences apparently of God**—experiences which seem to the subject to be experiences of God. (The phrase 'religious experience' has been used to describe a wide variety of experiences. I am confining it for present purposes to this sense.)

We may describe our experiences (perceptions) of things either in terms of what they are of; or—being careful in case we may be mistaken—in terms of what they seem or appear (general words), look, sound, feel, taste, smell (words which specify the sense involved) to be of. I may say that I perceive a desk, or just that I seem to perceive a desk, or that it seems (or since the sense involved is vision—that it looks) to me that there is a desk here. Note two very different uses of such verbs as 'seems', 'appears', and 'looks'. When I look at a round coin from an angle I may say that 'it looks round' or I may say that 'it looks elliptical', but I mean very different things by the 'looks' in the two cases. By 'it looks round' in this context I mean that—on the basis of the way it looks—I am inclined to believe that it is round. By 'it looks elliptical' in this context I mean that it looks the way elliptical things normally (that is, when viewed from above) look. The former sense in philosophical terminology is the epistemic sense; the latter sense the comparative sense. The epistemic sense of such verbs describes how we are inclined to believe that things are; the comparative sense describes the way things seem by comparing them with the way things normally seem. 'It looks blue to me' in the epistemic sense means that I am inclined—on the basis of the way it looks—to believe that it is blue; 'it looks blue to me' in the comparative sense means that it looks to me the way blue things look normally (i.e. in normal light).

An apparent experience (apparent in the epistemic sense) is a real experience (an apparent perception is genuine) if it is caused by that of which it purports to be an experience. My apparent perception of the desk is a real perception if the desk causes (by reflecting them) light rays to land on my eyes and thereby causes me to have the apparent perception.

Now it is evident that, rightly or wrongly, it has seemed (in the epistemic sense) to millions and millions of humans that at any rate once or twice in their lives they have been aware of God and his guidance. Surveys show that that is so for millions and millions today, let alone in past ages. (For the pervasiveness of religious experience, see David Hay, *Religious Experience Today* (1990), chapters 5, 6, and Appendix.)

They may be mistaken, but that is the way it has seemed to them. Now it is a **basic principle of rationality, which I call the principle of credulity, that we ought to believe that things are as they seem to be (in the epistemic sense) unless and until we have evidence that we are mistaken.** (I did not discuss this principle in Chapter 2, because I was dealing there only with the step from agreed publicly observed events to other things beyond observation. Here I am dealing with how we should assess our private experiences.) If it seems to me that I am seeing a table or hearing my friend's voice, I ought to believe this until evidence appears that I have been deceived. If you say the contrary—never trust appearances until it is proved that they are reliable—you will never have any beliefs at all. For what would show that appearances are reliable, except more appearances? And, if you cannot trust appearances as such, you cannot trust these new ones either. Just as you must trust your five ordinary senses, so it is equally rational to trust your religious sense.

An opponent may say that you trust your ordinary senses (e.g. your sense of sight) because they agree with the senses of other people—what you claim to see, they claim also to see; but your religious sense does not agree with the senses of other people (they do not always have religious experiences at all, or of the same kind as you do). However, it is important to realize that the rational person applies the principle of credulity before he knows what other people experience. You rightly trust your senses even if there is no observer to check them. And, if there is another observer who reports that he seems to see what you seem to see, you have thereafter to remember that he did so report, and that means relying on your own memory (i.e. what you *seem* to recall having heard him say) without present corroboration. Anyway, religious experiences often do coincide with those of so many others in their general awareness of a power beyond ourselves guiding our lives (though not so much in a more detailed awareness of the exact nature of God and of his particular purposes). If some people do not have these experiences, that suggests that they are blind to religious realities—just as someone's inability to see colours does not show that the many of us who claim to see them are mistaken, only that he is colour blind. Nor, again, does the fact that some of a group of travellers cannot see some object which they cannot reach mean that, if many of the group claim to be able to see it, they are mistaken. The more rational belief—in the absence of further evidence about the visual powers of the different travellers—is that the former do not have good enough sight. If three witnesses in a law court claim (independently) to have seen the suspect in some street at a certain time, and three witnesses who were in the street at that time claim not to have seen him, then—other things being equal—the court will surely normally take the view that the suspect was there, and that the latter three witnesses simply did not notice him. It is basic to human knowledge of the world that we believe things are as they seem to be in the absence of positive evidence to the contrary. Someone who seems to have an experience of God should believe that he does, unless evidence can be produced that he is mistaken. And it is **another basic principle of rationality, which I call the principle of testimony, that those who do not have an experience of a certain type ought to believe any others when they say that they do**—again, in the absence of evidence of deceit or delusion. If we could not in general trust what other people say about their experiences without checking them out in some way, our knowledge of history or geography or science would be almost non-existent. In virtue of the principle of testimony, there become available to those of us who do not ourselves have religious experiences the reports of others who do, and to which, therefore, we can apply the principle of credulity. In the absence of counter-evidence, we ought to believe that things are as they seem to be to other people; and we do, of course, normally so assume. We trust the reports of others on what they see unless we have reason to suppose that they are lying, or deceiving themselves, or simply misobserving. We ought to do the same with their reports of religious experience.

The principle of credulity states that we ought to believe that things are as they seem to be unless and until we have **evidence that we are mistaken. There are three kinds of such evidence. First** we may have evidence that the apparent perception was made under conditions for which we have positive evidence that perceptions are unreliable. If I claim to have read a page of a book at a distance of a hundred yards, you will rightly not believe me—because we know from experience that humans who claim to be able to read at that distance in fact cannot correctly report what is written (as we can check what was written by reading the page at a distance of one foot, where the observational reports of so many of us agree with each other). Likewise, apparent perceptions by subjects under the influence of such drugs as LSD are rightly discounted, because we have found them to be unreliable (by the fact of observations made by many others, not under such influence). Most religious experiences do not fall foul of this test. They are not made under the influence of drugs or in conditions in which we have any positive evidence that that kind of experience is unreliable.

Second, we may have evidence in the particular case that things are not as they seem to be. I may think I see a man carrying his head under his arm. Since all my knowledge of human capacities suggests that humans cannot do this, I rightly think that I am subject to hallucination. This is the background knowledge of how the world works which we have seen at work, earlier in this chapter, in assessing claims about particular public events. Similarly, experiences apparently of God ought to be discounted if we have strong positive evidence that there is no God. I emphasize 'strong'. If we could not trust our senses when they seemed to show us what otherwise on a slight balance of probability we had reason to believe not to be so, we would always remain the prisoners of what we initially believed. If a slight balance of my evidence suggests that you are in London today (e.g. you told me yesterday that you would probably go to London today) and then I seem clearly to see you in Oxford, I ought to believe my senses, to believe that you are in Oxford today (and so believe that you changed your mind about going to London). It is only if I saw you getting on the train and the train leaving, and then heard you phoning me from Westminster with Big Ben striking in the background, that I ought to doubt my senses when I seem to see you in Oxford. Likewise with religious experiences: if we have strong reason to suppose that there is no God, we ought to disregard our religious experiences as hallucinatory. But, in so far as the other evidence is ambiguous or counts against but not strongly against the existence of God, our experience (our own or that of many others) ought to tip the balance in favour of God.

Third, there may be evidence that the apparent experience was not caused—whether directly or indirectly—by the object purportedly experienced. If I think I see John alone in the arcade at a certain time and then it is shown that his twin brother was in the arcade at that time, that makes it quite likely that it was light rays emanating from the twin brother which caused me to have the experience, and that John was not involved in causing me to have the experience. So, if you could show that some religious experience did not have God among its causes, that would show that it was not a genuine experience of God. However, the only way to show that would be to show that there is no God; for, if there is a God, he sustains all the causal mechanisms which produce all our experiences. Maybe some religious experiences occur when people fast for a period. But that does not show that God was not involved in causing those who are fasting to have a religious experience; for if there is a God, it is he who causes that discipline of fasting to bring about the experience. The mere fact that some process plays a causal role in my having an experience has no tendency to show either that the experience is illusory or that it is genuine. A drug introduced into my eyes may either cause me to see what is not there, or to open my eyes to what is there. And, if there is a God, the latter is the way that disciplines of fasting or whatever which bring about religious experiences work.

So, in summary, in the case of religious experiences, as in the case of all other experiences, the onus is on the sceptic to give reason for not believing what seems to be the case. **The only way to defeat the claims of religious experience will be to show that the *strong* balance of evidence is that there is no God.** In the absence of that strong balance, religious experience provides significant further evidence that there is a God.

It might be said that only the religious have religious experiences. That is not always so; but it is true that it is almost invariably those who have had some prior acquaintance with a religious tradition who have religious experiences—for some the experience is the means by which the tradition becomes alive for them again. But that is hardly an objection: for anything, unless we know what a so-and-so is, we are unlikely to have an experience which seems to us to be an experience of a so-and-so. Only someone who knew what a telephone was could seem to see a telephone. You may learn what a telephone is either by someone showing you one, and then you can recognize the next one you see; or by someone giving you a description of one, and then you will be in a position to recognize one when you see one. With a religious experience (in our sense of one which seems to the subject to be an experience of God), the way we learn what an experience of God would be like is by the religious tradition giving us an understanding of what God is like. My Chapter 1 provides a formal description of what God is like, but the tradition with its stories of those who purportedly have encountered God fills out such formal description in more detail. Thereby we come to *begin* to understand what an experience of God would be like if we had one; and all we need is enough understanding to recognize an experience when we have one—we could not possibly give a full description of such an experience in advance, or indeed after the experience. (For a famous story of someone who could not recognize an experience of God for what it was until he was told something about God, see the story of the child Samuel in the Temple (1 Sam. 3).)

For collections of descriptions of some modern religious experiences, see some of the studies produced by the Religious Experience Research Unit, now called the Alister Hardy Research Centre (e.g. Timothy Beardsmore (ed.), *A Sense of Presence* (1977); (note that many, but not all, the experiences described in this volume are religious experiences in my sense). Some religious experiences are experiences which we have by having some other sensory experience. Just as I become aware of someone's presence by hearing a voice, or become aware of the door opening by feeling the draught, so some people become apparently aware of God by hearing a voice or feeling a strange feeling, or indeed just seeing the night sky. But occasionally perceptions do not involve any sensory element at all (any patterns in a visual field, noises, smells, and so on); one just becomes aware that something is so. The blind may become aware of the presence of the furniture, though they do not have a feeling by means of which they become aware of it; or we become aware of whether our hand behind our back is facing upwards or downwards, though there is no 'feeling' which tells us which it is—we just know. Analogously, some religious experiences are such that it seems to the subject that God is present although there is no sensation by which the experience is mediated.

In ordinary perception, when, as normally, sensations (visual, auditory, and so on) are involved, **we do not infer to the object we seem to see from the sensations which accompany the awareness**. I recognize my daughter just like that, not by observing some pattern of colour in my visual field and reasoning that it must be caused by my daughter. Indeed, I may be quite unable to describe the characteristic pattern of colour in my visual field when I see her. So likewise with an experience of God. One knows much more clearly what it is of than what are the sensations by which it is accompanied.

I suggest that **the overwhelming testimony of so many millions of people to occasional experiences of God must**, in the absence of counter-evidence of the kind analysed, **be taken as tipping the balance of evidence decisively in favour of the existence of God.** However, those who have such experiences agree only in respect of what they are aware of. Some of them claim that their experience gave them further information about the nature of God, or that he had told them to do certain things. And, just as even the claim that there is a God does need to have a certain degree of initial probability (on the basis of the evidence analysed in earlier chapters) in order that religious experience may be taken as genuine, so even more does any claim about what he is like or what he has done. Someone who claims that God has told them to commit rape must be mistaken, because we know on other grounds that rape is wrong and therefore God would not have commanded it.

The conclusion of this book is that the existence, orderliness, and fine tunedness of the world; the existence of conscious humans within it with providential opportunities for moulding themselves, each other, and the world; some historical evidence of miracles in connection with human needs and prayers, particularly in connection with the foundation of Christianity, topped up finally by the apparent experience by millions of his presence, all make it significantly more probable than not that there is a God.

EPILOGUE: SO WHAT?

I reach the end of this book with some dissatisfaction. I am well aware of objections other than the ones which I have discussed which can be made to almost every sentence which I have written. Some of these objections have been around for very many centuries; but for a modern book directed in part against the larger book of mine on which this short book is based, see J. L. Mackie's *The Miracle of Theism* (1982). I am also aware of counter-objections which can be advanced in turn against every objection to my views; and also of the need for qualification and amplification of most of the assertions in this book.

Argument and counter-argument, qualification and amplification, can go on forever. But religion is not exceptional in this respect. With respect to any subject whatever, the discussion can go on forever. New experiments can always be done to test Quantum Theory, new interpretations can be proposed for old experiments, forever. And the same goes for interpretations of history or theories of politics. But life is short and we have to act on the basis of what such evidence as we have had time to investigate shows on balance to be probably true. We have to vote in elections without having had time to consider the merits of the political programmes of even the main candidates with respect to one or two planks of their programmes. And we have to build bridges and send rockets into space before we can look at all the arguments for and against whether our construction is safe—let alone be absolutely certain that it is. And in religion too we have to act (while allowing that, later in life, we may look again at the arguments).

The conclusion of this book was that, on significant balance of probability, there is a God. If you accept it, it follows that you have certain duties. God has given us life and all the good things it contains, including above all the opportunities to mould our characters and help others. Great gratitude to God is abundantly appropriate. We should express it in worship and in helping to forward his purposes—which involves, as a preliminary step, making some effort to find out what they are. But duties are of limited extent (as we saw in Chapter 1); a moderate amount of worship and obedience might satisfy them. We could leave it at that. Yet, if we have any sense and any idealism, we cannot leave it at that. God in his perfect goodness will want to make the best of us: make saints of us and use us to make saints of others (not, of course, for his sake, but for ours and for theirs), give us deep understanding of himself (the all-good source of all being), and help us to interact with him. All that involves an unlimited commitment. But God respects us; he will not force these things on us—we can choose whether to seek them or not. If we do seek them, there are obvious obstacles in this world to achieving them (some of which I discussed in Chapter 6). The obstacles are necessary, partly in order to ensure that our commitment is genuine. But God has every reason in due course to remove those obstacles—to allow us to become the good people we seek to be, to give us the vision of himself—forever.

GUIDE TO FURTHER READING

Philosophy of religion is the examination of the meaning and justification of central religious claims (of other religions, as well as of Christianity). *Is There a God?* sought to provide what I believe to be the true answer to the central question of the philosophy of religion. Here are some suggestions of further reading for those who wish to explore this question more fully, as well as other issues closely connected to it. Two modern books arguing against the existence of God:

Nicholas Everitt, *The Non-Existence of God*, Routledge, 2004.

J. L. Mackie, *The Miracle of Theism*, Oxford University Press, 1982.

Two introductions to modern philosophical writing on the main questions of the philosophy of religion:

Michael J. Murray and Michael Rae, *An Introduction to the Philosophy of Religion*, Cambridge University Press, 2008.

Charles Taliaferro, *Contemporary Philosophy of Religion*, Blackwell Publishers, 1998.

There are many good anthologies of the philosophy of religion which contain extracts from writings of many different authors, both classical and modern, with different views on the main topics. Three suitable ones are:

Louis P. Pojman and Michael C. Rae, *Philosophy of Religion: An Anthology*, 5th edn., Wadsworth Publishing, 2008.

William Lane Craig, *Philosophy of Religion: A Reader and Guide*, Edinburgh University Press, 2002.

Chad Meister, *The Philosophy of Religion Reader*, Routledge, 2008.

For the description of the latest discoveries and speculations of modern physics, relevant to the arguments of Chapter 4, see:

Paul Davies, *The Goldilocks Enigma*, Penguin, 2008.

The topics discussed in *Is there a God?* are all ones about which I have written at much fuller length elsewhere. On the whole topic, see *The Existence of God* (Oxford University Press, 2nd edn., 2004.) On the nature of God (the topic of Chapters 1 and 3) see *The Coherence of Theism* (Oxford University Press, rev. edn., 1993) and *The Christian God* (Oxford University Press, 1994). On the general issue of what is evidence for what (the topic of Chapter 2), see *Epistemic Justification* (Oxford University Press, 2001). On the nature of humans (that they consist of body and soul) see *The Evolution of the Soul* (Oxford University Press, rev. edn., 1997). On the Problem of Evil (the topic of Chapter 6) see *Providence and the Problem of Evil* (Oxford University Press, 1998). On the issue of the relevance to religious faith and practice of arguments about the existence of God, see *Faith and Reason* (Oxford University Press, 2nd edn., 2005).

INDEX